SpringerBriefs in Education

SpringerBriefs on Key Thinkers i

Series Editors

Paul Gibbs, Middlesex University, London, UK

Jayne Osgood, Middlesex University, London, UK

Labby Ramrathan, School of Education, University of KwaZulu-Natal, Durban, South Africa

This briefs series publishes compact (50 to 125 pages) refereed monographs under the editorial supervision of the Advisory Editor, Professor Paul Gibbs, Middlesex University, London, UK; Jayne Osgood, Middlesex University, London, UK; and Labby Ramrathan, University of KwaZulu-Natal, Durban, South Africa. Each volume in the series provides a concise introduction to the life and work of a key thinker in education and allows readers to get acquainted with their major contributions to educational theory and/or practice in a fast and easy way. Both solicited and unsolicited manuscripts are considered for publication in the SpringerBriefs on Key Thinkers in Education series. Book proposals for this series may be submitted to the Editor: Nick Melchior E-mail: Nick.Melchior@springer.com

More information about this subseries at https://link.springer.com/bookseries/10197

Karin Murris

Karen Barad as Educator

Agential Realism and Education

 Springer

Karin Murris ⓘ
Faculty of Education
University of Oulu
Oulu, Finland

School of Education
University of Cape Town
Cape Town, South Africa

ISSN 2211-1921   ISSN 2211-193X (electronic)
SpringerBriefs in Education
ISSN 2211-937X   ISSN 2211-9388 (electronic)
SpringerBriefs on Key Thinkers in Education
ISBN 978-981-19-0143-0   ISBN 978-981-19-0144-7 (eBook)
https://doi.org/10.1007/978-981-19-0144-7

This Springer imprint is published by the registered company Springer Nature Singapore Pte Ltd.
The registered company address is: 152 Beach Road, #21-01/04 Gateway East, Singapore 189721,
Singapore

To Simon and to our love and friendship.

Acknowledgements

To have been invited to contribute to this series is a real privilege. Many human and nonhuman bodies have intra-acted with the writing of this book and have made it possible. Karen Barad's writing's, video presentations, memories of their visit to Cape Town and seminar, very early morning sunrises, excitement, anxieties of never finishing, toothache, iMac, cycling, Malou Juelskjær's visit to the University of Oulu in September and our many conversations, swimming in the river, sauna, the frosty air, the first snow (in September!), walks with Delilah, Simon's delicious experimental dinners, wine, sunsets on the balcony, Poppy, dust, etc. are all entangled in this book.

Threaded throughout this writing are the Slow reading groups Vivienne Bozalek and iii started some seven years ago and the ideas that belong to no one in particular, and to all of us all at the same time. We meet weekly and often two or three times a week, now in Zoom and communicate almost daily via Whatsapp groups (see www.decolonizingchildhood.org). In particular, iii would like to thank Vivienne Bozalek, Rose-Anne Reynolds, Joanne Peers, Theresa Giorza, Angela Molly Murphy, Joanna Haynes, Anya Morris, Veronica Mitchell, Carole Scott, Hilary Janks, Barry Lewis, Aaniyah Omardien, Lieve Carette, Susie Taylor-Alston, Jill van Dugteren, Kerryn Dixon, Lynn Chambers, Judy Crowther, Meghan Judge, Sara Stanley, Sumaya Babamia, Magda Costa-Carvalho, Esther Pretti, Norma Rudolph, Nora Saneka, Luzia de Souza, Heloisa da Silva, Francois Jonker, Stefan Smit, Karen Barad, Annika Slabbert, Niike Romanos, Gustavo da Costa Bastos, Siddique Motala, and so many more!

Many thanks to Malou Juelskjær for travelling from Copenhagen to Oulu (despite the pandemic) and spending very precious and memorable days with us. Her three-day seminar for our doctorate students and staff and with Astrid Schrader as a guest speaker profoundly changed and deepened my understanding of agential realism. This event was funded by the University of Oulu through a special grant.

Chapter two has also greatly benefited from the dis/continuous engagement with data co-created during the research project *Children, Technology and Play* (CTAP), funded by the LEGO Foundation. Thanks to Joanne Peers, Theresa Giorza, Kerryn Dixon, and Chanique Lawrence for our im/possible task to do justice to our rich work with the children in the Western Cape and Gauteng. Thanks also to all the members of our audience when presenting these ideas at conferences and seminars in 2021 and their invaluable responses. Of course, without the hospitality of the children, teachers, and principals of the schools involved in the CTAP project, Chapter three and all the ideas the research generated would never have existed. My deep thanks for their generosity and patience, especially during the pandemic.

iii would also like to thank Tuure Tammi, in particular, for our inspiring teaching together this year at the University of Oulu and the students whose ideas feature in Chapter four. This would not have been possible without them and the guest lecturers on the course: Walter Kohan, Joanna Haynes, Riku Välitalo, Karen Malone, and Jayne Osgood.

iii would like to thank the following people for their permission to publish images. Karen Barad for giving permission to have a photo published from their Facebook profile (Figure 2.1). Brandan Reynolds for his permission to publish a screenshot from our co-created cartoon The Posthuman Child Manifesto (Figure 4.1). Karen Malone for her permission to publish a video clip (Figure 4.2). And Tuure Tammi for his permission to publish the soundscape of our students' "choir" (Figure 4.3). Contributed to this research has been the funding of the National Research Foundation of South Africa. Grant number: 442658.

A special thanks to Simon Geschwindt for his unwavering support and the editing of this book. With love.

Oulu, November 2021

About This Book

This book is about becoming touched and moved by Karen Barad's agential realism. *Karen Barad as Educator* is not biographical. It is not *about* Barad. There is much to be learned about teaching and education research through the human and other-than-human narrative characters in Barad's writings and way of life. Reading this book is about becoming entangled with, and being inspired by, a passionate yearning for a radical reconfiguration of education in all its settings and phases (e.g., not only day-care centres, schools, colleges, universities, but also homes, museums, or therapy rooms). This book will appeal to lecturers, teachers, artists, therapists, parents and grandparents, funders of education research, organisers of educational events, as well as detached youth workers. In short, this book will speak to anyone interested in the 'what' and the 'how' of educational encounters and who is interested in alternatives to the dominant neoliberal national curricula, educational policies, and humanist teaching, research, and conference agendas. The book aims to offer a gripping account for educators to be inspired by the invigorating and elusive philosophy of agential realism with a specific focus on iterative performative practices that profoundly matter to what counts as knowledge, teaching, learning, and response-able education science.

Contents

List of Figures

List of Tables

Chapter 1
Troubling the Troubled Subject

1.1 The World Kicks Back

It might come as a surprise that a book with the title *Karen Barad as Educator* is not a "typical" narrative account of the person, their work, and their life. Instead, in a gesture to trouble human-centrism, this book involves becoming touched and moved by Barad's agential realism through narratives that include other-than-human characters without erasing Karen Barad as subject nor other humans. Agential realism acknowledges how the human is always already implicated in knowledge-making practices.[1] Reading this book involves getting entangled with the ethics and politics of what it means to know, teach, and learn. It also reveals what is involved in researching or reading and writing a book adopting agential realism as a philosophy. The use of extensive quotes is deliberate. They are a material attempt to make Barad present in their absence. Learning 'about' their philosophy of agential realism is enacted through the ways in which Barad writes, talks, listens, and engages with worldly be(com)ings.

Teaching and learning take place not only in day-care centres, schools, colleges, or universities but also at home, on the beach, in museums, in the slaughterhouse,[2] or in the therapy room. This broader notion of education includes so-called formal and informal educators such as lecturers, teachers, artists, therapists, parents, and grandparents, funders of education research, organisers of educational events, such as seminars and conferences, as well as detached youth workers who work with people on the streets, and many more. In short, this book speaks to anyone interested in the

---

[1] Already in 1995 (p. 65), Barad writes about their dismay 'that many physicists continue to use phrases that imply that properties are observer-independent attributes of objects-even in texts on quantum mechanics'. In other words, Barad's posthumanism is not about decentring the human.

[2] See e.g., Helena Pedersen's fascinating and haunting posthumanist work with veterinary students (2013).

© The Author(s), under exclusive license to Springer Nature Singapore Pte Ltd. 2022
K. Murris, *Karen Barad as Educator*,
SpringerBriefs on Key Thinkers in Education,
https://doi.org/10.1007/978-981-19-0144-7_1

'what' and the 'how' of educational encounters and who is interested in alternatives to the dominant neoliberal national curricula, educational policies, and humanist teaching, research, and conference agendas. The book aims to provide a gripping account and unusual opportunity for educators to be inspired by the invigorating and elusive philosophy of agential realism. This introduction describes how its four chapters, including this one, aspire to do this and why it matters.

Agential realism is a philosophy *practised*, not a philosophy *applied* to practice. It is an *entangling* theory–practice affair. The philosophy troubles all boundaries that human language has put in place as indeterminate and treats them as not given beforehand (a priori). This book is not a cookie-cutter approach to methodology and pedagogy—a how-to-*apply*-agential realism guide. Philosophising is about generating *thinking as doing* without ready-made products to be regurgitated or applied. Nor is philosophical enquiry 'just' about process.[3] Disrupting any process–product duality, my diffractive engagement with agential realism hopes to inspire—and to inspire hope for justice-to-come[4]—by making fresh connections with every "new" reading.

Posthumanist pedagogies and research methodologies entail a special relation with truth without holding firm beliefs and taking up determinate epistemological positions. This philosophical attitude is one of the collaborative enquiries, thinking aloud together, generating cascading questions, embracing silence, and taking deep breaths in "temporary resting places". These epistemic places are dynamic and characterised by epistemic modesty by withholding claims to absolute truths. Rather than focussing on final answers, as so much of our educational systems require us to do (see, e.g., our assessment apparatuses), philosophical enquiry examines our relation with truth and celebrates questioning, the questions we ask and do not ask (Haynes & Murris, 2012). Epistemic modesty is, of course, not the same as embracing epistemic, cultural, or moral relativism (Chap. 3.1). It is certainly not the case that 'anything goes'. The 'world kicks back', not in the sense of individualised agency but agency as 'distributed over nonhuman as well as human forms' (Barad, 2007, pp. 214–215).[5] It is not individual bodies but intra-actions that are agentic (Barad, 2007, p. 184).[6]

---

[3] See Murris (2017) for my response to Gert Biesta's claim that Philosophy with Children (Chap. 4.3) is about process, thereby introducing the notion of learning as "worlding".

[4] See Chap. 3.8 and Chap. 4.

[5] Unlike Judith Butler's notion of 'performativity', for Barad (2007, p. 184) performativity is 'iterative intra-activity'.

[6] An agential realist reconfiguration of agency in educational research is at the heart of Chap. 3.

1.2 "We"

The book's engagement with Barad's work is iterative[7] and intra-active. It is an intense and dynamic adventure that leaves distinct traces of mattering, sedimenting the world as "we" go along. Barad's philosophy-physics profoundly *matters*. Environmental educators argue that *'our* very lives and the existence of our earth ecosystems depend on this work' (Brown et al., 2020; my emphasis). As Gan et al., (2017, p. G5) put it poignantly, it might be the 'horror of our civilization', but '[o]ne method is to notice that the "we" is not homogeneous: some have been considered more disposable than others'. There is no universal "we". With a focus on the (post)human, new feminist materialist Rosi Braidotti (2018, p. 23) argues that:

'We' – the dwellers of this planet at this point in time – are interconnected, but also internally fractured. Class, race, gender and sexual orientations, age and able-bodiedness continue to function as significant markers in framing and policing access to normal 'humanity'.

As I am writing,[8] wildfires sweep Turkey. Droughts, freshwater shortage, storms, and floods have become dramatically more commonplace. With ice caps melting, chronic diseases, contaminations, and pandemics as the global order of the day, it is becoming increasingly clear that these environmental crises do not affect all lives in the same way nor have they been produced equally (Tammi, 2019, p. 2). Thus, the "we" and "us" grammatically referred to in this book don't refer to a 'unified entity of humankind', but to 'a diverse and very unevenly enacted multiplicity, always constituted through processes of differentiation' (Juelskjær et al., 2021, p. 20).

Posthumanist (including agential realism) and new materialist fields of enquiry are characterised by their conceptual creativity. The reason for this is that "new" ways of thinking and doing require new terms. These grammatical changes are more than mere rhetoric. They articulate philosophies and theories that break with engrained anthropocentric practices and habits of thought that have led to climate change, unspeakable cruelty, extinction of nonhuman species, colonialist violence, extractivism, and widespread epistemicide (Murris, 2021).

Inspired by Donna Haraway's use of 'trouble' (see below), this book profoundly troubles and unsettles the humanist subject that has been the cause of so much trouble. Geologists claim that 'our' time is that of the Anthropocene, a human-damaged planet (Crutzen & Stoermer, 2000). Advanced industrial capitalism and colonialism, the mechanisation of labour, the extraction of fossil fuels, and the standardisation of global time have put "the human" on a linear timeline of progress. Education has been turned into an individualised, teleological humanising project, whereby humans and other beings have become an economic resource, obscuring collaborative survival (Snaza, 2015, pp. 26–27; Tsing, 2015, p. 19).

Agential realism pulls the rug from under our established educational assumptions about human agency, causality, intentionality, and voice. However, agential realism's

---

[7] See Astrid Schrader's important point that iterability (for Derrida) does not assume linear time (in Juelskjær et al., 2021, p. 52).

[8] When writing the first version of this text, the con/text was as described. See further below about the troubling of unilinear time-sequences.

decolonising work is not destructive, although it might be experienced like that at first. A certain amount of destruction is necessary for construction, like an engineer 'who "blasts" things in the process of building them' (Barad, 2017c, p. 23). It reminds me of a visibly upset student who commented that my posthumanist teaching 'had pulled the stop out of his bath'. He continued: 'now all the water is gone and there is nothing left in its place'. It shocked me at the time. Perhaps it would have helped him if I had pointed out that it is not about what is *in* the bath, but that we need to turn our attention as educators to the bath itself? This powerful bath-container metaphor provokes more questions. What is inside and outside this container, the measuring apparatus (Chap. 3), that holds the water? Who is the "we" that decides what is in the bath and counts as the body of knowledge worth having? "Inside" and "outside" are critically important concepts in education. Agential realism draws our attention to the philosophical assumptions and binaries that are *already in place* in educational practices before teaching or research projects get off the ground. Education is riddled with ontological metaphors that shape the content, outcomes, objectives, and pedagogical relations (Murris, 1997, 2016). This book aims, not to clarify or simplify and make agential realism 'easy', but to disturb how "we" humans tend to take binaries as given in education research and teaching, including *troubling* what and who "we" are as humans. Donna Haraway's use of "troubling" is inspiring. From the French *troubler*, the verb 'troubling' means 'to stir up', 'to make cloudy', and 'to disturb' (Haraway, 2016, p. 1). And this includes the concept "human".

Our ability as humans to 'look forward' has become entangled with what it means to be human, a so-called superior species, set ontologically apart from and above nonhumans in the order of things (Tsing, 2015, p. 21). For Haraway, the solution does not lie in trying to make an imagined future safe, but to stay with the trouble by 'learning to be truly present' (Haraway, 2016, p. 1). In this way, our own selves as humans are at stake. Troubling the troubled subject, Barad says in an interview that what 'we' (humans) do, think, and choose ('our' agential cuts) matter epistemologically, ontologically, ethically, aesthetically, and politically—yet:

> at the same time, there is no "we" that stands outside the intra-action deciding and choosing to make cuts; for this would be to assume a liberal conception of the (human) subject, which is being similarly problematized here along with the nature of objects and their assumed cut between "object" and "subject". "We" neither preexists nor is external and separable from what is iteratively delineated and remade. (Barad & Gandorfer, 2021, p. 25)

The "we" is not only human but an entangled 'zoo of subatomic particles' (Barad, 2007, p. 354). What the human as concept signifies is of critical importance in education. Education would not exist without it, and the human would not exist without education. They mutually constitute each other. At least since Plato, education has been 'a practice of humanisation undergone by the human', with the human as 'both a beginning point (an ontological given) and an end point (something one becomes through education) (Snaza, 2013, p. 41). As ontologically already given *and* the end product of education at the same time, the concept 'human' is deeply political because education 'structurally introduces the necessity of intermediate concepts: the less human, the less than fully human' (Snaza, 2013, p. 41).

1.3 Intra-active Relationality

The ontology of agential realism is not just relational (because many other conceptual frameworks are too) but also *intra-active*. Unlike the more familiar concept of inter-action, intra-action does not assume that things exist (e.g., me, the coffee cup, and my chair) before they are in relation with each other (as the concept of 'interaction' implies) (Barad, 2007, p. 184). Intra-action is a neologism—introduced by Donna Haraway (1992) and intra-actively developed by Karen Barad. Its spelling expresses a relational ontology. 'Intra', derived from Latin, means 'within', 'interior', and 'during'. At the heart of Barad's philosophy of agential realism, intra-action applies not only to subjects but also to objects. Intra-action 'signifies the mutual constitu-tion of infinitely entangled agencies' (Barad, 2007, p. 33) or what they (Barad) call *phenomena* as the 'basic units of existence' (Barad, 2007, p. 333). Phenomena are an 'ontological primitive'—not things, bodies, subjects, or objects (Barad, 2007, p. 429, ftn 14). The profound implications for education of this ontological move(ment) away from object ontology are illustrated and enacted throughout this book.

An effort has been made to articulate intra-active relationality as much as possible in both its form and content. Moreover, the writing or "genre" troubles the very distinction between form and content as well. For example, the intra-active relation "between" me and my own hard copy of the book *Meeting the Universe Halfway* is also materialised here in "my" writing. Read repeatedly for several years, mostly with peers during a weekly reading group,[9] the book opens itself at certain pages when picked up. Several pages from the index have fallen out and serve as bookmarkers. My attention is caught by yellow and pink highlighted text and my scribbled notes in the book. On pages 248 and 249, the paper is lightly stained and touched by hands, coffee, tea, sweat, and sand. The binding has given way:

> I argue that Bohr's reliance on human concepts, human observers, and human knowledge practices undermines his ability to offer a cogent interpretation. I then propose an interpreta-tion that is more faithful to naturalism than Bohr's. In particular, I propose an interpretation

---

[9] Since 2014, we have been meeting weekly: postgraduate students, colleagues (from various universities), and with anyone who is interested in reading texts about postqualitative enquiry, new materialism, and critical posthumanism. The reading group started as part of a research project funded by the South African government (National Research Foundation) between 2016 and 2018: *Decolonising Early Childhood Discourses: Critical Posthumanism in Higher Education* research project, but membership is now broader, open to the public and since COVID-19 is only online. We now connect via Zoom and keep in touch via Facebook and Whatsapp. Members are often interested in the way we read philosophical texts very slowly (Chap. 2.5). https://www.decoloniz ingchildhood.org/reading-group.

of quantum physics based on agential realism. In summary, in this chapter I **present a new scientific result**: a way of interpreting quantum physics that builds on Bohr's interpretation while removing its humanist elements. (Barad, 2007, p. 248; my emphasis)

'I present a new scientific result'. Intriguing. What on earth (and beyond) could quantum physics teach educators? Intra-actively entangled, I am struck again (and again) by the power of Barad's extraordinary writing and the significance of their philosophy, also for education. Quantum physics is no walk in the park (and neither is poststructuralism by the way; Barad, 2007, p. 249), but that is not where the main difficulty lies. Indeed, embarking on Barad's journey through the foundational issues of quantum physics is neither singular nor straightforward, but the main difficulty lies in how the results are counter-intuitive (Barad, 2007, pp. 248–249). Of course, intuition is not "natural". "We"—some more than others—are educated into a particular ontoepistemology and ethics, depending on age, language, race, geopolitical location, and so on. Yet, despite the inherent complexity of agential realism, Barad's influential is significant and especially the last 5 years their Google citations have risen dramatically: 22.341 citations in the last 5 years (Fig. 1.1).

In its design, Barad's philosophy-physics is a "magnus opus" (the implicit reference in the phrase to "master" (rather than *magna*) is unfortunate although typical in much of human language). Its core concepts include intra-action, quantum entanglement, erasure, phenomenon, indeterminacy, diffraction, agential cut, agential separability, and spacetimemattering. These create a philosophical and intra-actively connected network that *moves* aesthetically, epistemologically, politically, and ethically through its de(con)structing[10] ontology. Intra-actively related, Barad refers to the concepts ontology, epistemology, and ethics as 'ethico-onto-epistemology' (Barad, 2007, p. 409, ftn 10).

Karen Barad as Educator owes quite a lot to other books and articles which it is not competing with but with which it is entangled. Celebrating the invigorating and enlivening ongoing dialogues with other pathbreakers, in writing or otherwise, and building on their politically astute work, is a feminist academic practice. This book diffracts through Barad's scholarship with the spotlight on what we can learn from agential realism about pedagogy, education research, and organising educational events, such as seminars and conferences[11] (see, e.g., Chap. 4.3). The book also diffracts through other scholars who have regularly engaged with Barad's work, including those who have been and still are highly critical of agential realism. Their critiques have left material traces in my own dynamic understandings of agential realism. In an important sense, the use of the demonstrative pronoun "this" in "this book" is also deceiving because agential realism troubles modernist spacetime

---

[10] See above about destruction and construction, and for the methodology of de(con)struction in teaching. See in particular Chap. 4.

[11] 'This' book *Karen Barad as Educator* draws in particular on Barad's pedagogical engagements (Barad, 1995, 2000, 2013; Barad & Gandorfer, 2021; Juelskjær et al., 2021; Reardon et al., 2015) and their later writing on time, colonialism and de(con)struction as relevant for de/colonising education, and imaginaries for different futures (Barad, 2017a, 2017b, 2017c, 2018, 2019). Of course, it would be impossible to leave out their seminal work *Meeting the Universe Halfway: Quantum Physics and the Entanglement of Matter and Meaning* (2007).

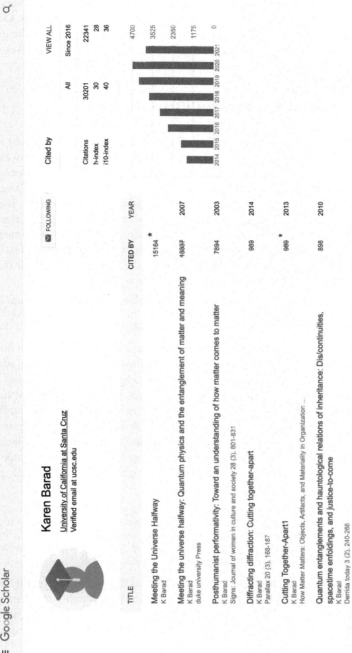

Fig. 1.1 Citations counts of Karen Barad's publications (*Source* Google Scholar [7 November 2021])

topologies that fix individual things in a particular location (Chap. 4). This book is iteratively and intra-actively constituted and entangled with me the author, my computer, my toothache, the river Oulu, snow, $-27\,°C$, university practices, Delilah the dog and Poppy the cat, the dust, you the reader of this book, concepts, the mould on the walls, future floods, the UN Convention of the Right of the Child, and so on.[12]

1.4 *Doing* Education and Life Differently

Agential realism is not just a philosophy. Not that philosophies are only about ideas. But like other new materialist and posthumanist orientations, agential realism explicitly theorises the significance of materiality in social and cultural practices. And not just at a theoretical level. It involves a profoundly different *doing* of research, and reading and writing texts through the provocative use of grammar. But not just academic texts. This book engages the reader with the radical implications for education when embracing agential realism personally as well as professionally. It is impossible to separate teaching from research, the personal from the professional, the domestic from the public, or the political from the academic. Agential realism troubles the Cartesian Subject in its core and 'all the way down':

> to the very atoms of existence, and beyond, to a point where individuality is itself undone by the specific entanglements of becoming that transcend the distinctions between bios and technics, organic and inorganic, artificial and natural, mind and body. (Barad, 2007, p. 362)

Barad explains in an interview how their writing style is not just an aesthetic choice, a literary device, a form of play, or merely a way of being creative. The genres adopted draw attention to the materiality of knowing, meaning-making, and writing itself (Juelskjær et al., 2021, p. 133). It is for this very reason that (again) in this volume, I have dared to make the familiar 'I' unfamiliar by using 'iii' (see also Murris, 2016). It deliberately causes trouble in reading, in a similar way to Barad's grammatical use of 'they', 'their', and 'them', instead of 'she' and 'her' in recent publications. This draws attention, not only to gender-neutral language but also to the need to move away from singular pronouns. As Barad (in Barad & Gandorfer, 2021, p. 30) explains:

> Let me emphasize again the difficulty of speaking, and using personal pronouns, such as "I." It would be incorrect to assume that there is an "I" that decides on choosing where to make a cut. This is a humanist flattening out of what I am trying to articulate. In intra-acting there is no distance between the "I" and "the world." There is no "I" that acts from the outside; rather, it is intra-actively constituted through practices of sense-making.

The un/doing of the individual self who writes or reads this writing as a matter of fact (*and* value) is entangled with a troubling of the self as an individualised determinately bounded and propertied human subject (Barad, 2007, p. 171). The subject itself has been put at stake throughout this book. Why is this important generally and especially

---

[12] See Chap. 3 for what is involved in tracing a subject or object as a phenomenon in its specificity.

in education? In what way do educators reinforce a particular notion of the subject through pedagogical and research practices?

The self is always deeply implicated in exclusionary boundary-making practices. Barad's invitation is to consider the 'material forces' that are 'contributing to the reiterative materialisation of this "I"?'. They ask: 'Which political forces and texts that I was reading helped constitute "me"?' (Barad in Juelskjær & Schwennesen, 2012, p. 11).[13] Each reading of the I is an iterative re-membering of the difficult task involved in troubling the troubled subject (see above). Reminiscent of Deleuze and Guattari's consciousness as not singular, but a pack of wolves,[14] Barad says that 'each "individual" is always already a crowd (and not merely in a psychological sense)' (Barad & Gandorfer, 2021, p. 60). An individual is not more than one because of how they feel or sense it (e.g., psychologically), but because their existence is such that relations have brought them intra-actively into existence. But not as an origin story. There are no beginnings nor endings.

The next three chapters examine the profound implications of this ontological shift from I to iii for education using a series of "knots".

1.5 Knotting

Another way this book troubles a self-present subject, a singular, separate 'I', is by its structure, woven together through *knots*. Carol Taylor and Simone Fullagar (2022, p. 73) propose that 'knots knit together, forge and sustain relations, enfold and connect'. The different knots in each chapter work diffractively, like waves overlapping, not progressively. There are no key arguments that run from the beginning to the end in straight lines. There is no linear logic that explains each concept before introducing the next. On the other hand, they are not randomly placed either. Each knot is in chapters with clear threads. You can start with it, yet it also follows on from what has gone before it. The knots are not things, but waves—bodies without

---

[13] But it does not imply that I cannot speak in the first person, according to Barad: 'After all the notion of an individual needs to be taken seriously—very seriously these days, because, for one thing, it is a very potent notion at the center of the action of neoliberal forces. At the same time, it's crucial to raise the question of how "the individual", including any particular individual, is iteratively (re)constituted' (Barad in interview in Juelskjær & Schwennesen, 2012, p. 11).

[14] Quoted from "my" book *The Posthuman Child* (Murris, 2016, p. 3): 'Gilles Deleuze and Felix Guattari, both highly critical of psychoanalysis, reject the idea of mind spaces, such as the unconscious as singular ("one Wolf"), a unity:

> How stupid, you can't be one Wolf, you're always eight or nine, six or seven. Not six or seven wolves all by yourself all at once, but one wolf among others, with five or six others…Freud tried to approach crowd phenomena from the point of view of the action of the unconscious, but he did not see clearly, he did not see that the unconscious itself is fundamentally a crowd. (Deleuze & Guattari, 2014, pp. 32–33)

The unconscious is a "crowd"; it is multiple, not singular. You can't say '*I am this, I am that*' (Deleuze & Guattari, 2014, p. 33)'.

determinate boundaries. In coming together, they are more than the sum of their parts, creating 'superpositions'.[15] Reading this book might be more like swimming or hopping than cycling or walking.

Tim Ingold (2013, p. 132) argues that knots are not like nodes in a network. Instead, they create *a lively meshwork*. Inspired by the work of French philosopher Gilles Deleuze, he writes poetically:

> Knots are places where many lines of becoming are drawn tightly together. Yet every line overtakes the knot in which it is tied. Its end is always loose, somewhere beyond the knot, where it is groping towards an entanglement with other lines, in other knots. What is life, indeed, if not a proliferation of loose ends! It can only be carried on in a world that is not fully joined up, not fully articulated. (Ingold, 2013, p. 132)

Of course, when re-turning to the "same" text, or knot, each reader will make different connections, including me as the author (as illustrated above). With each reading, the text *is* different as a matter of fact (and value). This is not because of what I bring to it in terms of meaning, but because the world that includes humans like me, will have moved on, literally. Even mountain ranges move on (Barad, 2014, p. 168), especially when influenced by climate change.[16] Movement of all bodies, human, and other-than-human is reconfigured. Space and time are not 'preexisting theaters for the play of things—movement does not happen within such a space and time' (Barad in Barad & Gandorfer, 2021, p. 55). According to agential realism, matter is agentive and a generative dynamic intra-active becoming: 'in the sense of bringing forth new worlds, of engaging in an ongoing reconfiguring of the world' (Barad, 2007, p. 170).

Knowledge can be stable and unchanging only within a deep dualist ontology where mind and matter as substances are seen as grounds for all that is and are part of different worlds (Murris, 2016, Ch. 1). Readers anticipating clarity and guidance about what they can learn from Barad about education will be disappointed. Knots are hospitable and performative, but they do not instruct or explain. 'One' knot is even deliberately left "empty": a k/not—making room for hopping into an ontology of 'no/thingness' (*hauntology*; Barad, 2019). The knots have been composed by reading Barad's writings and multimedia posts diffractively through pedagogical concepts, theories and "my" memories of pedagogical practices and experiences. Within each knot, citations (or part of them) are repeated, often with different emphases as a way of learning through re-turning—sedimenting the world in its iterative becoming. Like a game of hopscotch, this pedagogical playful ploy breaks with a forward linear movement of reading and slows it down. The knots are an invitation for the reader to diffract through their experiences, knowledges, dreams, and collective memories. The collection of knots is more than the sum of its total, a 'gathering' Anna Tsing

---

[15] The "coming together" is not the coming together of individual entities with determinate properties as in the concept of "mixture". Good examples of articulating the difference between superposition and mixture are "transdisciplinary" v "multidisciplinary" and "transmodality" v "multimodality". Superpositions embody quantum indeterminacy (Barad, 2007, p. 265).

[16] See e.g., https://phys.org/news/2015-11-climate-mountains.html.

(2015, p. 23) might say, and thinking with the knots will bring about unpredictable 'happenings' through 'contamination' (p. 27):

> We are contaminated by our encounters; they change who we are as we make way for others. As contamination changes world-making projects, mutual worlds—and new directions—may emerge. Everyone carries a history of contamination; purity is not an option.

Shae Brown et al. (2020) argue how Baradian agential realism could be a game-changing path in environmental education. When faced with the challenge of presenting at a conference of the Australian Association for Environmental Education (AAEE) Conference, they considered how to do it differently and why this was important:

> In planning the [90 minute] workshop, we sought to enact emergent conditions in which participants could embody knowledge to apply in their own work and/or life context. We were not there to present rhetoric, or explain what we 'knew', but to open our own learning and re-learning, our diffractive relationality with Barad's work and each other, to a collective engagement with other environmental educators and researchers, and indeed also with the other-than-human phenomena that also existed in that space. With the understanding that we are always already entangled, and that the boundaries between 'knower' and 'known' are not fixed, we hoped that the conversation would act to open the possibilities for response-ability with/to each other's being and becoming, learning and knowing, as environmental educators, researchers, colleagues. (Brown et al., 2020, p. 3)

As a presenter at conferences, the practice of disrupting binaries that imply knowing qualitatively better (e.g., more mature, abstract, and figurative) and quantitatively more is a refreshing change that troubles developmentalist notions of progress. It is rare for conference presentations to assume that the presenter is a learner as well as an "expert". In their writings and talks, Barad often behaves as though they are not an expert.

1.6 Karen Barad the Expert?

After presenting their seminal paper *Diffracting Diffraction: Cutting Together Apart* (2014) at a seminar in Cape Town, South Africa,[17] Barad stipulates that diffraction is not about comparing or contrasting when they talk about, for example, Niels Bohr—a scholar central to their agential realism. Despite extensively studying Bohr's work for decades, Barad claims surprisingly that they have no idea how to express what Bohr thought exactly. This is not because they find quantum physics too difficult to grasp

---

[17] This event was organised by the *Decolonising Early Childhood Discourses: Critical Posthumanism in Higher Education* project (DECD) (www.decolonizingchildhood.org). As Principal Investigator of this National Research Foundation of South Africa funded three-year project (2016–2019), iii were co-responsible for its organisation and we are currently co-writing and editing a book about the impact the event had, or better, still has on participants (Murris & Bozalek, forthcoming). The DECD project is still going strong and has been running Slow Reading groups since 2013, focusing mainly on Barad's publications. These weekly meetings are open to the public (see the website).

and understand. On the contrary, quantum physics and their diffractive reading of Bohr is at the core of their agential realism as the following disciplinary information in their biography attests:

> Karen Michelle Barad (born 29 April 1956), is an American feminist theorist, known particularly for their theory of Agential Realism. They are currently Professor[18] of Feminist Studies, Philosophy, and History of Consciousness at the University of California, Santa Cruz. They are the author of *Meeting the Universe Halfway: Quantum Physics and the Entanglement of Matter and Meaning.* Their research topics include feminist theory, physics, twentieth-century continental philosophy, epistemology, ontology, philosophy of physics, cultural studies of science, and feminist science studies.
>
> Barad earned their doctorate in theoretical physics at Stony Brook University. Their dissertation presented computational methods for quantifying properties of quarks, and other fermions, and in the framework of lattice gauge theory.[19]

Taking Bohr's ontology[20] seriously for Barad means that they need to consider whatever 'apparatus' they use to read Bohr with and the phenomena this creates. The apparatus is an inseparable part of the observed phenomenon (Barad, 2014, p. 180).[21] So, the analytical task is to read the *phenomenon* (Chap. 3.5), not Bohr's thinking, as though it existed outside the subject, the **I**, doing the reading. In the same vein, there is no Barad speaking in this book. To try and do so would have been an impossible task because as iii read Barad and re-read and reread their texts and re-turn to 2017 through recorded videos of the seminar, *what* iii read changes through the intrinsic intra-active relationality. The specificity of the apparatus[22] iii bring to it is entangled as part of the process of re-turning to the text: other theories, philosophies, practices, experiences, past, presents and futures, and especially our weekly reading groups.[23] Re-turning is not only reading in the narrow sense but also includes the process of writing—a better word for this intra-active process might be "composing" through "composting". In conversation with Martha Kenney (in Davis & Turpin, 2015, pp. 258–259), Barad's inspiration, friend, and colleague Donna Haraway proposes 'com-post', instead of 'post-human':

> The Anthropocene has had a conflicted etymological history. A number of experts think of anthropos as "the one who looks up from the earth," the one who is earth-bound, of the earth, but looking up, fleeing the elemental and abyssal forces, "astralized." "Human" is a better figure for our species, if we want a species word, because of its tie to humus, compost. Unlike anthropos, humus is not about looking up; it's about being hot. [Laughter] Beth Stephens and Annie Sprinkle have this little bumper sticker "compost is so hot," for one of their feminist ecosexual slogans. It's not post-human, but com-post. Katie King has been playing with the

---

[18] In 2021, Karen Barad is Distinguished Professor, not Professor.

[19] From: https://www.goodreads.com/book/show/15916941-what-is-the-measure-of-nothingness-infinity-virtuality-justice-was.

[20] See Chap. 3.8 about the reworking of "ontology".

[21] Barad (2014, p. 180): 'This is direct evidence of Bohrian complementarity: wave and particle are not inherent attributes of objects, but rather the atoms perform wave or particle in their intra-action with the apparatus.'

[22] See Chap. 3.2.

[23] See https://www.decolonizingchildhood.org/reading-group.

term "composting humanities," and Rusten Hogness came up with "humusities" to replace "humanities." "Homo" needs to re-root in humus, not bliss out into an apocalyptic anthropos. Compost provides the figures for making multispecies public cultures, sciences, and politics now.

Writing, composing, composting through re-turning to texts of any kind disrupt notions of expertise in a human body (in this case, that of Karen Barad). Following from the dynamism of indeterminacy, the past in all its materiality is open, not closed (Chap. 3.6). This includes my turned over, com-posted, disintegrating, Barad autographed, hard copy of *Meeting the Universe Halfway*. For an agential realist, learning is never completed; it is always ongoing and part of the ongoing materialisation and reconfiguring of the world (Barad in Juelskjær et al., 2021, p. 123). Of course, this includes learning about agential realism too. Both learning as engaging in worlding and agential realism as a philosophy are continuously changing and developing (but not progressively from "less" to "better" or "more mature"). Much posthumanist research in education is a footnote to Karen Barad's agential realism.[24] This book helps to navigate some of the key philosophical terms that are now so well established that a recent publication with the title *Dialogues on Agential Realism: Engaging in Worldings through Research Practice* (Juelskjær et al., 2021) includes only one chapter by Karen Barad themselves.

Again, this book is not *about* Barad. And this book is not about *Barad*. The first would imply representationalism (see below); the second would assume ontological individualism and anthropocentrism. The title of this book, *Karen Barad as Educator*, gestures towards a decentring of the Subject as well as the Subject of the author of this book, "me". Agential realism is read diffractively through educational science in the way iii engage with education as a porous diffracted body. *Karen Barad as Educator* is my intra-active reading of Barad's scholarship as well as their enacted pedagogical practices diffractively through education.[25] Barad puts this reluctance to claim any kind of expertise beautifully in the context of their knowledge of Niels Bohr[26]:

> I have no idea how to say what Bohr thought exactly, and I don't think that Bohr would want me to say what Bohr was thinking because if I take Bohr seriously in terms of his ontology, whatever apparatus I used to read Bohr with, it's not going to be separate from—in other words it forms its own phenomena and the best I can do is describe the phenomenon. Now the way that I read Bohr has changed as I have studied him over the decades, so I'm reading different things while I'm rereading Bohr and rereading Bohr and rereading Bohr. So, Bohr is being read already through Foucault as I'm reading Foucault, and Foucault is always already being read through Bohr, and many other people and many other texts. The apparatus has many different dimensions to it but I can't possibly fully articulate, so this is not a compare and contrast exercise in the usual way. I'm sure there are creative things that people can say about compare and contrast, but not the kind of high school exercise that we were given which is like, 'here's what so and so said, and here's what so and so said, and now compare them'.

---

[24] See e.g., the *Glossary* (Murris, 2022).

[25] iii are inspired here by what Karen Barad says about their expertise in terms of my expertise about education.

[26] During a seminar in Cape Town. See Footnote 17.

The influence of Jacques Derrida[27] is unmistakable in much of Barad's agential realism, especially their later writings,[28] including the idea that there is no fixed, stable meaning of any text. In turn, Derrida himself was an avid reader and drew on many academic philosophers, including German philosopher Martin Heidegger. The quote from Barad above is inspiring to diffract through:

> I have no idea how to say what Barad thought exactly, and I don't think that Barad would want me to say what Barad was thinking because if I take Barad seriously in terms of their ontology, whatever apparatus I used to read Barad with, it's not going to be separate from—in other words it forms its own phenomena and the best I can do is describe the phenomenon. Now the way that I read Barad has changed as I have studied them for almost a decade, so I'm reading different things while I'm rereading Barad and rereading Barad and rereading Barad. So, Barad is being read already through Heidegger as I'm reading Heidegger, and Heidegger is always already being read through Barad, and many other people and many other texts, such as those by Christine Battersby, Jane Bennett, a plant leaf, Anthony Browne, stingrays, Erica Burman, Lewis Carroll, Leonard Cohen, giving birth, Gilles Deleuze, the national curriculum, Rene Descartes, hospitable atmosphere, John Dewey, Rose Braidotti, my watch, Kieran Egan, Miranda Fricker, the waves in Muizenberg, *The Posthuman Child Manifesto*, Roger Greenaway, miscarrying, Joanna Haynes' nose, Mark Johnson, Eliana, *The Constant Gardener*, Immanuel Kant, childing with Walter Kohan, George Lakoff, my shopping list, Matthew Lipman, Loris Malaguzzi, Gareth Matthews, Martha Nussbaum, *Me and my Bellybutton*, Maurice Sendak, the key hole, Hillevi Lenz Taguchi, pencil, Brandan Reynolds, bellybuttons, Plato, university policies, Hans Zimmer…

iii are not comparing Barad with Heidegger and other thinkers and texts, but the diffractive *gathering*—always more than the sum of its total—draws attention to the fact that a text *is* already context, better expressed as *con/text*.[29] The following gem is "hidden" in another footnote (Barad, 2007, p. 459, ftn 62):

> "Contextual" is not a particularly apt term. The notion of context connotes separability as a starting point: it presumes there is an object that exists apart from its environment or surroundings and that this environmental context matters in some way.

The distinction between "text" and "context" is profoundly structuring in education—a power-producing binary that includes and excludes. Children and students' behaviour and performances are evaluated based on their socio-economical, cultural, and geopolitical contexts. Education research tends to work with nesting scales between local (e.g., home, school), regional, national, and global. For some time,

---

[27] For a helpful podcast on Jacques Derrida, see: https://www.bbc.co.uk/sounds/play/m000nc7t and 38.40 min in about Derrida's rejection of the stable meanings of texts. Barad was unusual in their interest in Derrida. In an interview, they explain: 'I remember mentioning Derrida at a lunch with my physics colleagues at Colombia in the mid-80s. It was immediately evident that I had committed the ultimate faux pas, and that in any case no one had any idea what I was talking about. So much for C.P. Snow' (Barad in Juelskjær & Schwennesen, 2012, p. 11).

[28] Very much inspired by their doctoral researcher Astrid Schrader. See Barad's tribute to Schrader: 'The title of my essay [*On touching: The inhuman that therefore I am*; 2012] here expresses my virtual engagements and entanglements with Derrida. I am indebted to Astrid Schrader and Vicki Kirby for putting me in touch with Derrida through their marvelous materialist readings of his work' (Barad, 2012, ftn 1).

[29] For Barad's use of the forward slash, see Chap. 3.8.

especially in qualitative research practices, it has not been the capital "I" that centres our research practices, but the "ii". The neologism 'ii' (Murris, 2016) expresses the self in context or relation with the other (e.g., the environment, other humans, or my cat). But the 'other' here is understood as a separate autonomous entity. Categories of self-in-relation are 'nested' within each other like Russian dolls. But this kind of research separates child ontologically from her 'context'.

In contrast, the posthuman self ('iii') is always already in relation, a porous, 'unzipped' watery body consisting of nonhuman matter, drinking, leaking, weeping, pooing, and always already connected with the other (Neimanis, 2017). In agential realism, these "nesting" relationships are not understood as geometrical, but as topological manifolds (Barad, 2007, p. 246), and are 'intra-actively produced through one another' (Chap. 4.1). These and other agential realist ideas are genuinely mindboggling. It is difficult not to get overwhelmed by their generative possibilities and not get lost in their complexities.

1.7 Getting Lost

Meeting each knot offers different entry points for collective thinking-with (Haraway, 2016, Epigraph 2, p. 173). As Donna Haraway puts it, thinking-with is a kind of thinking that enlarges the capacities of all players (human and other-than-human) 'beyond inherited categories and capacities, in homely and concrete ways' (Haraway, 2016, p. 7). Taken together, these knots do not give an overview, not even a partial picture of what can be said about Barad as educator. They are connected and separate at the same time and eschew wholeness and boundedness. The knots are material ways of sedimenting the world—an agential force in its iterative differential becoming (Barad, 2007, pp. 180–181). Although Barad uses the concept of sedimentation regularly, it might give the wrong impression of solidity, fixedness, permanence, or immobility. The point is not that time leaves a mark (e.g., on bodies) as the external force of change; becoming is not an unfolding in time but an ongoing dynamic process of differentiation. 'Sedimenting does not entail closure' (Barad, 2014, p. 168).

The knots are invitations and provocations for readers to make fresh and unexpected connections. The making of new worlds is always already in relation with the other-than-human (Tsing, 2015, p. 22). It involves a giving up of trying to *master* the world through our grasping and colonial knowledge-making practices of capturing a world "out there". As Barad puts it materially in a footnote:

> I don't intend to capture an idea but to evoke further thought: Imagine putting drops of colored dyes into a piece of bread dough. As you knead the dough, the dyes spread out in different patterns of entangled lines and surfaces. But this process is too tame as well, since the changes are all continuous and the dough maintains its topology. So break off some pieces and reattach them to different areas and continue kneading. Take a different kind of dough and make a different manifold with different lines, surfaces, and volumes of color. Intermingle the dough pieces: new entanglements form, new possibilities emerge. This metaphor still doesn't cut it; the motion seems to come from the outside, the indeterminacies don't appear to be evident, the possibilities come across as less lively, fresh, and exuberant

than they are. Instead of dough, consider … other possibilities … in an unending iterative process of enfolding. (Barad, 2007, p. 439, ftn 85)

Getting lost is part of the joy and frustration of a philosophical education, especially for adults whose identities depend on knowing certain things more than other people. Educators are usually taught that knowledge acquisition involves transmitting entire bodies of knowledge that can be mastered by individual selves. Teacher education still operates based on either realist or socio-constructivist and constructionist ontologies (Chap. 3). Nonetheless, I hope that the reader will sense a kind of warm homecoming and that their educational practices will resonate with agential realism or at least with some of the pedagogical ideas this book points towards. After all, changing how we do our education and research is a necessary condition for the iterative process of de/colonisation—educational projects increasingly on the agenda in higher education and closely connected to a Derridean inspired de(con)struction (Chap. 3.6 and Chap. 4). Posthumanism makes a pledge to the still missing peoples of humanism; however, as argued elsewhere, child and childhood are seldom mentioned even in the posthumanist literature as missing peoples (Murris, 2021, Ch. 3). Thinking-with is a philosophical education—a childlike[30] education where questions are met with more questions opening up collaborative philosophical enquiries (Chap. 4.3). It is here that I situate my own scholarship: *meeting academic philosophy and pedagogy halfway.*[31]

What are the radical implications of Barad's scholarship for teaching and learning, and how can the reader take response-ability for encountering these new ideas? That is the question, and it is with a felt sense of urgency iii invite the reader to engage with the knots in this book diffractively, not as individualised conscious acts, by reflecting and rehearsing how educational theory and practice can be changed in the abstract, but through their own changed practices in their specificity. Each of the three chapters starts with an introduction that sets out some core ideas, followed by knots that can be read linearly but also in any order because each concept is intertwined with others. So perhaps the knot that catches the eye the most in terms of making a felt connection—or when the book has been used often on whatever page it opens up—is the one to start with. In each knot, there will be cross-references to others in this book. Each offers a different concept inspired by Barad's complex philosophy-physics. A concept is not abstract but a material-discursive practice provoking new imaginaries of doing (higher) education.

The knots are diffracted through by Karen Barad's complex writing, texts that include audio podcasts, videos, critiques of Barad's scholarship, interviews, art performances and an event—a seminar when they visited Cape Town in 2017.[32]

---

[30] Child as concept is complex and refers to chronological, fleshy child in spacetime, as well as the abstract notion that exists only because of its polar opposite, that is, adult. A childlike pedagogy is ageless, and proposing it is a form of political activism (see especially Chap. 4).

[31] This particular use of the phrase is of course inspired by Karen Barad's influential book entitled *Meeting the Universe Halfway* (main title) (2007). Quantum physics and queer theory are 'partnered all the way down' writes Haraway (2016, p. 33) about Barad's book title.

[32] See Footnote 17.

This book is not about transmitting and informing the reader about the right way of reading Karen Barad's agential realism, a Truth to follow, a theory to embrace, leading to the right way of teaching or doing education research. Instead, the four chapters diffract through one another and constitute an educational response; how might "we" as educators respond response-ably to Barad, and to each other—differently aged humans and other-than-human? How can this academic intimacy touch the right nerve, materially and discursively, to imagine other ways of doing education, more in/humane,[33] without the dichotomies always already in place. What are the crutches for education when un/doing[34] the power-producing binaries that have crippled how humans relate to each other in education and to the other-than-human? How can Karen Barad as educator help us re-imagine a nonviolent world in all its materiality that is a little bit easier to love[35]?

With courage and trepidation iii diffract through Karen Barad's extraordinary scholarship. Through their lively enactment of their profound philosophy, Barad encourages us to diffract critically without the "usual" criticality (Chap. 4). Barad (in Barad & Gandorfer, 2021, p. 31) invites us to walk around in our conceptual distinctions, continually re-think and re-do our concepts and practices (which of course are entangled anyway) and 'without taking these distinctions to be foundational or holding them in place' (Barad, 2012, p. 124).

The chapters in this volume take up this exciting challenge as an open invitation. Karen Barad lives their philosophy-physics. They are not just modelled as a theoretical example for us to copy. Every one of us needs to do that work in our own way and response-ably in our everyday life as academics (Chap. 2), as education researchers (Chap. 3) and teachers in schools and universities (Chap. 4). There are no founding Fathers (or Mothers), to follow, to copy, or to emulate. In that sense, we are epistemological orphans (Braidotti, 1991) and homeless nomadic subjects. But we are not alone. Other earthlings, large and small, are the condition of our existence. There is no measure of scale that precedes our intra-actions.

Diffracted through one another, the chapters inspire a different doing of teaching, learning, and education research. Hopefully, its celebration of the birth of a new kind of realism that is non/representational and intra-actively relational affects you with a profound sense of why the ontoepistemological shift matters ethically and politically. Its main aim is to offer imaginaries for radically de/colonising educational futures without prescription, romanticising, or moralising. Barad's writing diffracts through the academic writing, presentations, poems, and novellas produced by philosophers, poststructuralist, and postcolonial thinkers, women of colour, feminist colleagues, and friends (e.g., Gloria Anzaldúa, Judith Butler, Jacques Derrida, Michel Foucault, Donna Haraway, Kyoko Hayashi, Trinh Minh-ha, Walter Benjamin). Barad also diffracts through more unusual, other-than-human characters: the brittle star,

---

[33] See Chap. 3.8 for the Baradian use of the forward slash.

[34] Binaries cannot be undone as if this were an ideal future state, hence the use of the forward slash—see Chap. 3.8.

[35] A remark philosopher of childhood Walter Kohan made when we were co-presenting at a conference.

queer atoms, the void, slime moulds, stars, lightning, constellations, crystals, frogs, Frankenstein, and virtual particles. In turn, while diffracting through Barad's scholarship in *Karen Barad as Educator*, be prepared to meet plastic bricks, the moon, an aquarium, Zuko, a pregnant stingray, Facebook, a stick, ghosts, and many other kin. They are analysed, not as objects or things in the world, but as phenomena. Articulating those stories might help "stretch" our response-ability as educators to include *all* humans and other-than-humans as part of our earthly survival and more just futures.

References

Barad, K. (1995). A feminist approach to teaching quantum physics. In S. V. Rosser (Ed.), *Teaching the majority: Breaking the gender barrier in science, mathematics, and engineering* (pp. 43–75). Teacher's College Press.

Barad, K. (2000). Reconceiving scientific literacy as agential literacy, or learning how to intra-act responsibly within the world. In R. Reid & S. Traweek (Eds.), *Doing science+ culture* (pp. 221–58). Routledge.

Barad, K. (2007). *Meeting the universe halfway: Quantum physics and the entanglement of matter and meaning.* Duke University Press.

Barad, K. (2012). On touching: The inhuman that therefore I am. *Differences: A Journal of Feminist Cultural Studies, 23*(3), 206–223. https://doi.org/10.1215/10407391-1892943

Barad, K. (2013). Ma(r)king time: Material entanglements and re-memberings: Cutting together-apart. In P. Carlile, D. Nicolini, A. Langley, & H. Tsoukas (Eds.), *How matter matters: Objects, artifacts, and materiality in organization studies* (pp. 16–31). Oxford University Press.

Barad, K. (2014). Diffracting diffractions: Cutting together-apart. *Parallax, 20*(3), 168–187.

Barad, K. (2017a). Troubling time/s and ecologies of nothingness: On the im/possibilities of living and dying in the void. *New Formations: A Journal of Culture/Theory/Politics.* Special Issue on Posthumanist Temporalities, M. Rossini & M. Toggweiler (Eds.), *92,* 56–86.

Barad, K. (2017b). No small matter: Mushroom clouds, ecologies of nothingness, and strange topologies of spacetimemattering. In A. Lowenhaupt Tsing, H. A. Swanson, E. Gan, & N. Bubandt (Eds.), *Arts of living on a damaged planet: Ghosts and monsters of the Anthropocene* (pp. G103–120). University of Minnesota Press.

Barad, K. (2017c). What flashes up: Theological-political-scientific fragments. In C. Keller & M.-J. Rubenstein (Eds.), *Entangled worlds: Religion, science, and new materialisms* (pp. 21–88). Fordham University Press.

Barad, K. (2018). Troubling time/s and ecologies of nothingness: On the im/possibilities of living and dying in the void. In M. Fritsch, P. Lynes, & D. Wood (Eds.), *Ecodeconstruction: Derrida and environmental philosophy* (pp. 206–248). Fordham University Press.

Barad, K. (2019). After the end of the world: Entangled nuclear colonialisms, matters of force, and the material force of justice. *Theory & Event, 22*(3), 524–550.

Barad, K., & Gandorfer, D. (2021). Political desirings: Yearnings for mattering (,) differently. *Theory and Event, 24*(1), 14–66.

Braidotti, R. (1991) *Patterns of dissonance: A study of women in contemporary philosophy* (E. Guild, Trans.). Polity Press.

Braidotti, R. (2018). A theoretical framework for the critical humanities. Special Issue: Transversal Posthumanities. *Theory, Culture & Society.* Advanced online publication. https://journals.sag epub.com/doi/full/10.1177/0263276418771486

Brown, S. L., Siegel, L., & Blom, S. M. (2020). Entanglements of matter and meaning: The importance of the philosophy of Karen Barad for environmental education. *Australian Journal of Environmental Education*, 1–15. https://doi.org/10.1017/aee.2019.29

Crutzen, P. J., & Stoermer, E. F. (2000). The "Anthropocene." *Global Change Newsletter, 41*, 17–18.

Deleuze, G., & Guattari, F. (1987/2014). *A thousand plateaus*. Translated and a foreword by B. Massumi. Bloomsbury.

Donna Haraway in Conversation with Martha Kenney. (2015). Anthropocene, capitalocene, chthulhocene. In H. Davis & E. Turpin (Eds.), *Art in the Anthropocene: Encounters among aesthetics, politics, environments and epistemologies* (pp. 255–271). Open Humanities Press.

Gan, E., Tsing, A. I., Swanson, H., & Bubandt, N. (2017). Introduction: Haunted landscapes of the Anthropocene. In A. Tsing, H. Swanson, E. Gans, & N. Bubandt (Eds.), *Arts of living on damaged planet* (pp. G1-14). University of Minnesota Press.

Haraway, D. (1992). The promises of monsters: A regenerative politics for inappropriate/d others. In L. Grossberg, C. Nelson, & P. A. Treichler (Eds.), *Cultural Studies* (pp. 295–337). Routledge.

Haraway, D. (2016). Staying with the trouble: Making kin in the Chthulucene. Duke University Press.

Haynes, J., & Murris, K. (2012). *Picturebooks, pedagogy and philosophy*. Routledge.

Ingold, T. (2013). *Anthropology and/as education*. Routledge.

Juelskjær, M., Plauborg, H., & Adrian, S. (2021). *Dialogues on agential realism: Engaging in worldings through research practice*. Routledge.

Juelskjær, M., & Schwennesen, N. (2012). Intra-active entanglements: An interview with Karen Barad. *Kvinder, Køn & Forskning, 21*(1–2), 10–23.

Murris, K. (1997). *Metaphors of the child's mind: Teaching philosophy to young children*. Ph.D. thesis, University of Hull.

Murris, K. (2016). The posthuman child: Educational transformation through philosophy with picturebooks. In G. Dahlberg & P. Moss (Eds.), *Contesting early childhood series*. Routledge.

Murris, K. (2017). Learning as 'worlding': Decentring Gert Biesta's 'non-egological' education. *Childhood & Philosophy, 13*(28), 453–469. https://doi.org/10.12957/childphilo.2017.29956

Murris, K. (Ed.). (2021). *Navigating the postqualitative, new materialist and critical posthumanist terrain across disciplines: An introductory guide* (pp. 135–150). Routledge.

Murris, K. (Ed.). (2022). *A glossary for doing postqualitative, new materialist and critical posthumanist research across disciplines*. Routledge.

Neimanis, A. (2017). *Bodies of water: Posthuman feminist phenomenology*. Bloomsbury.

Pedersen, H. (2013). Follow the Judas sheep: Materializing post-qualitative methodology in zooethnographic space. *International Journal of Qualitative Studies in Education, 26*(6), 717–731.

Reardon, J., Metcalf, J., Kenney, M., & Barad, K. (2015). Science & justice: The trouble and the promise. *Catalyst: Feminism, Theory, Technoscience, 1*(1), 1–36.

Snaza, N. (2013). Bewildering education. *Journal of Curriculum and Pedagogy, 10*(1), 38–54. https://doi.org/10.1080/15505170.2013.783889

Snaza, N. (2015). Toward a genealogy of educational humanism. In N. Snaza & J. A. Weaver (Eds.), *Posthumanism and educational research* (pp. 17–30). Routledge.

Taylor, C., & Fullagar, S. (2022). In K. Murris (Ed.), *A glossary for doing postqualitative, new materialist and critical posthumanist research across disciplines* (pp. 72–73). Routledge. https://www.routledge.com/A-Glossary-for-Doing-Postqualitative-New-Materialist-and-Critical-Posthumanist/Murris/p/book/9780367484699

Tsing, A. L. (2015). *The mushroom at the end of the world: On the possibility of life in capitalist ruins*. Princeton University Press.

Tammi, T. (2019). What if schools were lively more-than-human agencements all along? Troubling environmental education with moldschools. *Environmental Education Research*. https://doi.org/10.1080/13504622.2019.1584881

Chapter 2
Meeting Karen Barad: An Agential Realist Life

2.1 Introduction: 'How Can I Be Responsible for That Which I Love?'

Karen Barad's love of physics has driven their life and work. Strikingly formulated through the question, *'How can I be responsible for that which I love?'*, Barad explains their motivation to read texts by poststructuralists, Continental philosophers, and queer theorists and to learn discourses that are unfamiliar to a natural scientist:

> I realized that I was going to have to train myself to think with folks in the humanities and social sciences if I wanted to get closer to the burning questions of justice and science that kept me awake at night. (Juelskjær et al., 2021, p. 120)

The title of their book, *Meeting the Universe Halfway: Quantum physics and the Entanglement of Matter and Meaning* (2007), expresses Barad's diffractive reading of the natural and social sciences. It is at the heart of the intra-active re-working from within physics to counter and interrupt the very practice of doing science and its violent histories (Chap. 3). Karen Barad starts their monograph as follows:

> This book is about entanglements. To be entangled is not simply to be intertwined with another, as in the joining of separate entities, but to lack an independent, self-contained existence. Existence is not an individual affair. Individuals do not preexist their interactions; rather, individuals emerge through and as part of their entangled intra-relating. Which is not to say that emergence happens once and for all, as an event or as a process that takes place according to some external measure of space and of time, but rather that time and space, like matter and meaning, come into existence, are iteratively reconfigured through each **intra-action,**[1] thereby **making it impossible to differentiate in any absolute sense between creation and renewal, beginning and returning, continuity and discontinuity, here and there, past and future.** (Barad, 2007, p. ix; my emphases)

---

[1] Intra-action is not only about a change from 'presumed separability to nonseparability (relational ontology) but entails a radically different understanding of causality and an ontoepistemological framework with implications for thinking about questions of justice' (Barad, 2017a, p. G119, ftn 17). See also Chap. 1.

© The Author(s), under exclusive license to Springer Nature Singapore Pte Ltd. 2022
K. Murris, *Karen Barad as Educator*,
SpringerBriefs on Key Thinkers in Education,
https://doi.org/10.1007/978-981-19-0144-7_2

   This is the opening paragraph of Barad's most influential book to date (2007). This gem of a paragraph is a stock cube of the entire book, and re-turned to throughout this chapter. Interestingly, it is in the Preface, which readers of books often skip (as they do with footnotes). It is the materiality of the discursive that (also) matters. For example, Appendix A takes up Alice Fulton's poem *Cascade Experiment* in its entirety (Barad, 2007, pp. 397–398), but two sections of the poem in *Meeting the Universe Halfway* appear materially distanced from each other (at the beginnings of Chaps. 1 and 8). The *place* of the poem itself in the book disrupts classical notions of causality as continuous and linear. Barad explains:

> …there is more to causality than the runaway scenario that unfolds in deterministic fashion. Dominoes are surely not what Alice Fulton had in mind in her poem "Cascade Experiment," with its ethico-onto-epistemic attention to our responsibilities not only for what we know but for what may come to be. A **cascade** in Fulton's sense is not a serial chain of consequences, an inevitability set in motion by some initial act, but **an iterative reconfiguring of possibilities entailed in our passional advances toward the universe**. (Barad, 2007, pp. 263–264; my emphases)

Like the jewels to be found in the footnotes of their published writings, reading Barad's oeuvre is like a treasure hunt and the verb of 'cascading' is only one of its many treasures. The verb enables a postdevelopmental working with questions that cascade when tracing phenomena (enacted in Chaps. 3 and 4). Barad's writing is intra-active, trans-layered, diffracting the personal and the professional, as well as disciplines through one another. In a preliminary note to the footnotes to Chapter 8 of *Meeting the Universe Halfway* (2007, p. 466; my emphases), Barad playfully apologises to Fulton for cutting up her poem:

> My apologies to Alice Fulton for placing passages of her magnificent poem "Cascade Experiment" at what seems to be a considerable distance from one another. At least I have done so in good faith; for even a cut that breaks things apart does not cause a separation but furthers the entanglement! My hope is that the reader will understand these seemingly separate passages not as bookends framing the beginning and end of the book, or mere echoes of each other, but rather as an entangled state that **reworks notions of contiguity and identity** much as a poem does not so much touch our lives here and there, offering us individual moments of reflection, but rather **gets inside our skin and reworks who we are**.

The cutting up is an *agential* cut that does not separate and cut into two parts like a Cartesian cut does (Chap. 3.8). Instead, it furthers the already existing relationalities: a 'cutting together-apart' in one move (Barad, 2014). As an agential cut, Barad's philosophy reworks who "I" *am* and who Barad *is*. Their scholarship works in unexpected affective ways through questions that cascade infinitely.[2] Being affected is more than emotion or feelings; it is a mutual performativity that troubles cognition/emotion, nature/culture, and inner/outer binaries (Barad, 2007).

   As the book's subtitle *Quantum physics and the Entanglement of Matter and Meaning* suggests, one of its key ideas is that matter and meaning are not ontologically separate. In a sense, maybe its first sentence 'This book is <u>about</u> entanglements'

---

[2] See, for example, how the cascading of questions works in the examples of diffracting practices in Chaps. 3 and 4.

Karen Barad

Fig. 2.1 Meeting Karen Barad on Facebook. (October 2021—created with their own photo.) Published with the kind permission of Karen Barad

could be re-written as "This book is <u>within</u> entanglements". Human writing is part of a relational world-making process in all its ongoing materiality, even without the human. Matter and meaning do not exist independently from one another. Not even from the outset.

For an agential realist, matter and meaning are not separate entities subsequently put into a relationship with one another by a human—interacting through notions such as causality or agency.[3] This would assign too central a vantage point, or knot hole, to the human author as being in charge (Master[4]) of the causal chain. The agential realist reconfiguration of the human, including Karen Barad themselves,[5] is beautifully "portrayed"—without a human face—in their Facebook profile (Fig. 2.1). Thrilled by how the photo had worked out,[6] and by diffracting it through the letters "Karen Barad", the image articulates the lively and dynamic naturalist ontology of agential realism (Rouse, 2004). The moon shines on 'the world's radical aliveness', and 'in an entirely non-traditional way, [agential realism] reworks the nature of both relationality and aliveness (vitality, dynamism, agency)' (Barad, 2007, p. 33).

The agential realist ontological re-working of relationality is a rejection of over-simplified and nonrelational notions of the human as a priori. Still, it does so *without claiming that the human doesn't matter!*[7] But, for Barad, the concept 'human' does not refer to individual things (objects) with inherent properties in the world, for example, with agency or with 'the ability to engage in cognitive functions that make

---

[3] See also Footnote 1.

[4] Replacing God, in the highest rung of the hierarchical species ladder that ascends from simple to complex, since the Enlightenment, Man as the Master (adult male, rational, able-bodied, and heterosexual) is at the top of the Great Chain of Being.

[5] See also Chap. 1 for Karen Barad's gender neutral and plural use of "they", "them", "themselves", and my neologisms "i", "ii", and "iii".

[6] From an email conversation with Karen Barad.

[7] See, e.g., the below quote about how humans participate in world-making. But not all world-making is done only by humans.

the universe intelligible' (Barad, 2007, p. 352). Re-turning to Alice Fulton's poem *Cascade Experiment,* and with a nod to Martin Buber,[8] Barad (2007, p. 354; my emphasis) argues that humans—like lizards and electrons—

> exist only as a result of, and as part of, the world's ongoing intra-activity, its dynamic and contingent differentiation into specific relationalities. "We humans" don't make it so, not by dint of our own will, and not on our own. But through our advances, we participate in bringing forth the world in its specificity, including ourselves. We have **to meet the universe halfway**, to move toward what may come to be in ways that are accountable for our part in the world's differential becoming. All real living is meeting. And each meeting matters.

2.1.1 Meeting the Universe Halfway

'Meeting the Universe Halfway' is not only the title of their influential 2007 book but also the title of Barad's 1996 publication. The earliest mentioning of agential realism can be found in 1995 in a chapter entitled *A Feminist Approach to Teaching Quantum Physics.* It is published in a book about breaking the gender barrier in teaching what we now call STEM (Science, Technology, Engineering, and Mathematics). These publications had an impact, initially on science studies scholars, such as Nelson and Nelson (1997), Mayberry (1998), and Biagioli (1999), and each publication attributes agential realism to Karen Barad.

Meeting the universe halfway is an ontological proposal for diffracting through the disciplines (transdisciplinarity) and *undisciplining* the disciplines we are so familiar with. In an interview with Malou Juelskjær and Nete Schwennesen (2021), Barad recalls "their" memories of past engagements across disciplines. Troubling unilinear time when narrating the past that is always open 'to future retellings (a point that resonates with insights from quantum theory as well)', Barad narrates some "auto" biographical details as follows:

> So there was a time, actually many times, as there still are, when I was reading all kinds of different things from different fields at once: physics, philosophy, science studies, feminist and queer theories, to name a few of my many debts. (Admittedly this is a rather unusual antidisciplinary omnivorous reading practice for someone with a career in physics, who grew up in the northeastern part of the US, just at the tail end of baby boom, postwar, post-Sputnik, a working-class second-generation American who was the first in my family to go to college, without any expectation of being an academic. My boundary crossing and indeterminate ways of being have never allowed me to fit any academic space comfortably. (Barad in Juelskjær & Schwennesen, 2012, p. 11)

Re-turning to the question 'How can I be responsible for **that** which I love?', for Barad, the 'that' in the question includes not only humans but also the other-than-human: matter, stars, moon, brittle stars, stingrays, queer atoms, reading texts through one another, and fields of enquiry such as physics. Notably, the 'that' does not signify objects and subjects in space and time as containers, but as intra-active *phenomena* (see especially Chap. 3). You will meet these phenomena in 'this' chapter and the

---

[8] See: Barad (2007, ftn 1, p. 466).

other chapters of this book. Intra-action[9] is about connectedness with the world. It assumes that, as individual humans, we have no control over the network of relations we always already find ourselves in and how they affect us. Humans can distance themselves from other subjects and objects only in abstraction (through human-made categories). This could be, for example, by using the concept "I", "woman", or "child". Importantly, relations are not something we (as humans) create.

Phenomena, not 'independent objects with inherent boundaries and properties', are *the primary units of existence*—the basis of a new ontology (Barad, 2007, p. 333) (See Chap. 1). The Baradian notions of quantum entanglement and phenomena trouble binaries at their core—even popular posthumanist distinctions between "human" and "nonhuman", "more-than-human", or "other-than-human". These highly differentiating boundary-making practices 'produce crucial materializing effects that are unaccounted for by starting an analysis after these boundaries are in place' (Barad, 2012a, p. 32).

So, for an agential realist, "this" book—*Karen Barad as Educator*—that you might be holding in your hand right "now" as you read "these" words—is not an object, but a phenomenon.[10] Meeting this book matters in the sense that it reconfigures teaching, learning, and education research by offering "zigzagging" possibilities to break with 'ladder thinking' (Heijnol, 2017, p. G96).[11] Meeting is a 'gathering': bringing about unpredictable 'happenings' (Tsing, 2015, p. 23).[12] Through a gathering of *knots*,[13] the book's structure is more like a game of hopscotch. You can hop in this chapter from one knot to the next, backwards, forwards, and sideways, including the option of hopping into other chapters and into 'no/thingness'—an "empty" k/not (Chap. 4). Intra-actively engaging with the text (in an unbounded sense of the word "text") may offer imaginaries for more just futures. Futures that are always iteratively in the making. This philosophical work does not proceed through linear rational

---

[9] See Chap. 1 for the "origin" of the neologism intra-action.

[10] iii are not suggesting that agential realism or 'being an agential realist' has a stable identity or essence that can be defined. It is a short-hand for certain onto-epistemological commitments to intra-active relationality that are always already ethical and political (see Chap. 1).

[11] As Andreas Hejnol powerfully summarises in the highly recommendable 2017 edited book *Arts of Living on a Damaged Planet* by Anna Tsing and colleagues: 'Genetic technologies have raised a suite of new questions about the ordering of organisms, and they have shifted the ways through which we understand evolutionary relations. They force us to rethink the anthropocentric notions of complexity, with their origins in ancient Greece, that continue to haunt biological thinking today. The figure of Aristotle's Great Chain of Being persists in the ongoing resistance to illustrating the actual evolution of sponges and urochordates. According to ladder thinking, comparatively complex animals should not come prior to simpler animals. But what, after all, is complexity? If there is such a thing as "complexity," it is an adaptation to specific ecological conditions, not the outcome of a teleological process. Furthermore, in any use of the term, complexity should not be defined as morphological or behavioral similarity to humans' (p. G96). Barad's chapter in this book called *No small matter: Mushroom Clouds, Ecologies of Nothingness, and Strange Topologies of Spacetimemattering* is particularly helpful as a condensed summary (stock cube) of their agential realism, in particular about the planetary politics inside an atom.

[12] See this chapter.

[13] For a detailed explanation of the knotted structure of this book, see Chap. 1.

argumentation (Barad, 2015, pp. 387–388), for example, by analysing and offering new definitions of concepts, nor, by rethinking the taxonomies and models we use to categorise objects and subjects (bodies in the world). Instead, agential realism starts somewhere else in the universe. It reworks Object and Subject altogether, ontologically.

Barad even says about their "own" book, *Meeting the Universe Halfway*, that 'it is not so much that I have written this book, as that it has written me. Or rather, "we" have "intra-actively" written each other', thereby reworking both what a "book" *is*, and an "author" *is* (Barad, 2007, pp. ix, x). These are bodymindboggling ideas that go against centuries of engrained Western habits of thought and require much unlearning (as a way of learning). How do agential realists rework the concepts we routinely think with and take for granted?

In a recent talk, Barad comments how 'sedimented ways of thinking … are so deep that we hardly question them anymore, both in physical theories, but also political theories …'. They suggest that 'it is not about finding something pure, but to keep the questions moving, **by always asking the prior question**'.[14]

2.2   On Entanglement

Intra-actively entangled with "my" writing and "this" book is the coronavirus pandemic.[15] The current grand narrative conflates the virus SARS-CoV-2 with the disease COVID-19 and, further, the pandemic. It frames the virus as an extraordinary threat outside "us" humans that needs to be overcome and eliminated. This is done, for instance, through disciplining bodies to comply with the demand to wear face masks, sanitise hands, physically distance, and be isolated for quarantining, medical care, and even death. It is also assumed that the virus is determinate and can be understood with epistemic certainty. SARS-CoV-2 can be mastered and controlled through human agency. The virus provokes many cascading questions about self-identity and health. COVID-19 is surrounded by additional stigma when someone "has" the disease, reflecting the discourse of undesirable bodies and connected with the politics of "personal" responsibility (e.g., the pressure to get vaccinated).

In a Question and Answer session[16] after their talk at *The Material Life of Time* conference in 2021,[17] Karen Barad makes an ontological connection with SARS-CoV-2. As Barad argues, individualism is typical of how the virus is regarded. Nations have responded with a highly problematic notion of nonrelationality already built

---

[14] See: https://www.youtube.com/watch?v=68I0y1koakA.

[15] See for the Ebola virus as a phenomenon: https://aabrahams.wordpress.com/2017/02/06/inter-intra-action-eng/. The video from the Three Minute Theory series called 'Intra-action' is embedded in the text.

[16] For the troubling of the pedagogy of Question & Answer sessions, see Chap. 4.3.

[17] This second International Conference of the Temporal Belongings Network was held online 15–17 March 2021. See: https://www.temporalbelongings.org/the-material-life-of-time.html.

into the concept of a person. This includes regarding individual bodies as units, including nations. At the time of writing, vaccinations are only available for certain affluent countries and not others. But—Barad continues—without taking our intra-dependency as an ontological given, it will be impossible to eradicate the virus in one nation if other nations remain unvaccinated.[18] The ontological shift from object or subject to phenomenon[19] is beneficial in thinking differently about how countries could deal with the pandemic.

The human-SARS-CoV-2 entanglement troubles "being" (*onto*) philosophically. For an agential realist, each cell, virus, and organism is a dynamic multiplicity of a host of others. We depend on one another "all the way down" (to micro-scales). Inspired by French philosopher Jacques Derrida, Barad (2019, p. 42) proposes that *difference* and not identity is the ontological starting point of relationality.[20] The pressing questions that cascade are: how could educators engage with the virus beyond a notion of difference that assumes identity as already given? Why does this matter, and for whom? Or, more provocatively, 'What would the coronavirus say to us if we asked it the right question?'.[21]

Throughout their scholarship, Barad communicates their unease about Euclidian mathematics[22] and Newtonian meta/physics, and, more broadly, all ontologies that take individual discrete existence as given, as in the concept of "interaction" and the use of personal pronouns, such as "I":

> It would be incorrect to assume that there is an "I" that decides on choosing where to make a cut. This is a humanist flattening out of what I am trying to articulate. In **intra-acting** there is no distance between the "I" and "the world." There is no "I" that acts from the outside; rather, it is intra-actively constituted through practices of sense-making. (Barad in Barad & Gandorfer, 2021, p. 30)

Sense-making, theorising, imagining, knowing, reading, writing, remembering, walking, critiquing, dressing, exercising, lesson planning, learning, mothering, and birthing—they are all *intra-active material-discursive practices* with/in the world.[23] Barad's diffractive engagement with quantum physics provides empirical[24] evidence for reworking the notion of entanglement as *quantum* entanglement.

---

[18] From Barad's talk *Infinity, Nothingness and the Un/doing of Self* during the Q&A part of the Summerschool 20 July at Cornell University: https://events.cornell.edu/event/karen_barad_infinity_nothingness_and_the_undoing_of_self.

[19] This is a similar shift as the one from **I** to iii. See: see Chap 1 and below.

[20] Barad (2019, p. 42) argues that all bodies (micro *and* macro) are unbounded by their skin, because each 'self' or 'individual' is already 'made up of all possible histories of virtual intra-actions with all others'.

[21] Sophie Wustefeld asked Vinciane Despret this in an interview (from: https://etopia.be/covid-19-vinciane-despret-il-va-falloir-apprendre-a-cohabiter-avec-le-virus/; transl. by S. Geschwindt).

[22] See e.g., Barad (2007, p. 376).

[23] As performative practices, they make a difference in world-making by entangling *and* differentiating as one move ('cutting together-apart') in the making of phenomena (Barad, 2015, pp. 5–6).

[24] For Barad's use of empirical, see especially Chap. 3.5.

> Quantum entanglements are not the intertwining of two (or more) states/entities/ events, but a calling into question of the very nature of twoness, and ultimately of one-ness as well. Duality, unity, multiplicity, being are undone. "Between" will never be the same. One is too few, two is too many. (Barad, 2014, p. 178)

The proposed reconfiguration of the numbers "1" and "2" has implications for what is, and is not, included in the concept of "entanglement" ontologically. The previous discussion of SARS-CoV-2 as an entanglement is an excellent example of why this matters. Are viruses part, or not part, of "identity"? (Sect. 2.3). A different arithmetic, a different ontology of numbers inspires 'a different sense of ac-count-ability ... a different calculus of response-ability' (Barad, 2014, p. 178). Agential realism resists pathologising and psychologising relationships with "others". By un/doing the very nature of matter, agential realism draws out the ontological conditions that make such performative practices of pathologising and psychologising possible. Philosophical assumptions about the existence of individualised bodies with insides and outsides have epistemological and also ethical and political implications. What would a different sense of 'ac-count-ability' and 'response-ability' bring about?

Agential realism is an open invitation to think and live intra-actively otherwise, both at the "personal" and "professional" level (and includes troubling the distinction "between" the "two"). Living intra-actively reworks what the (human) body *is* and what it can *do* by resisting existing categorisations, including making decisions ("agential cuts"[25]) about who and what belongs to specific entanglements. Concepts assume specific entanglements: "I", "we", "family", "community", "friendship", and so on. The concept of "family" is important in education and research (Murris, 2021a). It tends to be assumed that the concept 'family' is about humans related genetically and according to bloodlines—the people whose names or photos you would expect to see in a family tree. Nonmale line descendants are usually harder to find. When inviting student teachers to draw a family tree, they rarely draw their pet animals, although some draw adopted siblings or stepparents.

On one such occasion, our enquiries about the concept 'family' as non-hierarchical, without a root, trunk, and branches (like the tree metaphor of knowledge) cascaded into the concept 'pet animals', an outing to an aquarium and a botanical garden in Cape Town. In turn, these activities provoked encounters with rotating planets in Augmented Reality apps on smartphones, thereby making planets "alive" (Murris et al., 2018). Such transmodal pedagogies provoke students to ask profound questions about the hierarchy "between" human and other-than-human, thereby troubling anthropomorphism (prioritising human needs over animals and object). In our scientifically tidied up world in the hierarchical tree-like schema, the question "Who belongs to what?" is crucially important—possibly even a matter of life and death. People tend not to eat their pet animals or humans, but they do eat other animals. Donna Haraway (2016, p. 2) asks passionately:

> Who lives and who dies, and how, in this kinship rather than that one? What shape is this kinship, where and whom do its lines connect and disconnect, and so what? What must

---

[25] For the important agential realist notion of "agential cut", see Chap. 3.7.

be cut and what must be tied if multispecies flourishing on earth, including human and other-than-human beings in kinship, are to have a chance?

How does the concept 'family' work to include and exclude? Who is, and who is not, part of the (anthropocentric) family? The answer to this question critically matters for the ethics and politics of education (Hohti & Osgood, 2020).

As explored in more detail in Chap. 4, together with our student teachers we use a wide range of materials (part of the "family"!), such as light tables, fabric, string, paint, clay, paper, and tablets to discuss the exclusion of the "other" such as viruses and pet animals. But we also include those humans (also animals) who are still not considered as fully human because of their age, race, ability, class, gender, or sexuality (see, e.g., Murris, 2016, 2019, 2020, 2021; Murris & Borcherds, 2019a, 2019b; Murris & Muller, 2018; Murris & Somerville, 2021). Importantly, the playful pedagogies we enact are themselves intra-active material-discursive practices. This means the students learn *about* agential realism *through* the enactment of posthumanist ontologies (see Chap. 4). These pedagogies trouble engrained binaries in (higher) education, such as culture/nature, teacher/student, cognition/emotion, mind/body, collaborative/individual, and inside/outside. By their combined involvement in making sense, imagining, visiting, remembering, walking, and lesson planning together, the students' concept of "family" expands to include the other-than-human and the lesser-than-human. Students' reading of Karen Barad's work, watching their talks and the students' diffractive journal writing on Google drive (Murris, 2016), forms a different kind of kinship. This is not just a fanciful experiment. Teaching as a world-making practice plays a role in constituting who and what come to matter. It helps students appreciate that the past is never finished and that patterns of thinking are open to reconfigure futures, not only their own but also of those whose existence has not yet been noticed. The notion of quantum entanglement articulates our connections and responsibilities to one another.

In a moving tribute in the Preface of *Meeting the Universe Halfway* (2007), we meet Karen Barad's mother. We learn about Barad's passionate yearning for justice and its entanglement with the intra-active material-discursive practices of mothering and nurturing. Preferring not to thank individuals in the way authors usually do in the Acknowledgments section, Barad muses:

> I smile at the thought of imagining my mother reading this and thinking that I have made things unnecessarily complicated once again; that I have been thinking too much, and that anyone else would have just gotten to the point and said their thank-you's in a manner that all the people who have helped along the way could understand. On the one hand, she's right of course: what good is there in offering recognition that can't be recognized? But it is precisely because of the passionate yearning for justice enfolded into the core of my being-a passion and a yearning inherited from and actively nurtured by my mother-that I cannot simply say what needs to be said (as if that were a given) and be done with it. (Barad, 2007, p. x)

The driving force behind *Meeting the Universe* is a yearning for justice, that is enfolded into to core of Barad's being but is also larger than any individual (Barad, 2007, p. xi).

Returning to the question 'How can I be responsible for **that** which I love?' (Sect. 2.1), 'that' includes not only humans but also the other-than-human, through the transdisciplinary reading of texts through one another, including physics and queer theory. At the same time, agential realism resists pulling subjects and objects into categorisations (including the subject/object distinction), such as "family", and reworks these concepts as quantum entanglements. The notion of response-ability opens up more parts of the world to love.

2.3   On Identity

Barad does not reserve the yearning for justice for just the human. In response to a question after a keynote, Barad presents a fascinating argument:

> Yearning is not an anthropocentric notion. For example, in chemistry we talk about electrons wanting an extra one. Language of desire being evoked. Magnets with the same poles is materially felt in the body and when I switch them over you can feel they want to go together in a bodily sense. So why does the human have to own the concept of yearning? We already know what this yearning feels like in our bodies. Is it really that different whether humans want to be together or magnets want to be together?[26]

In this case, chemistry and physics provoke vital questions for social scientists. These questions linger and open up fresh and different possibilities for knowing, learning, and teaching. Does the human own the concept of identity? What are the theories that humans have invented to bring into existence human-centred notions of identity? These notions of identity privilege 'possessive individualism' over relationality as 'the template for explanation' (Haraway, 2016, p. 60). Although Barad's close colleague and friend Donna Haraway (2016, p. 190, ftn 10) refers here to biology when mentioning 'the dead ends of competition/cooperation binaries', it is not difficult to see the relevance for education. Carla Hustak and Natasha Myers argue that 'a zero-sum game based on competing methodological individualists is a caricature of the sensuous, juicy, chemical, biological, material-semiotic, and science-making world' (cited in Haraway, 2016, p. 68). Transdisciplinary enquiries are essential for troubling troublesome individualised explanations to enable a more 'fleshed-out description' (Haraway, 2016, p. 190, ftn 10).

Without a predetermined or fixed endpoint and as always in the making, theorising in agential realism[27] involves putting insights, practices, and 'whole' disciplines in conversation with one another, without silencing one over the other in research. In this case, it is the relevance of troubling individualism in biology (Haraway) and in quantum physics (Barad). Notably, the bodies that agential realists put in conversation are not bounded and homogenous but are always already entangled with other practices of knowing. Hence the encounter is from within, not without (Juelskjær et al., 2021, p. 124). More complex explanations and deciding what counts as "data"

---

[26] From: Karen Barad. *Infinity, Nothingness, and the Un/doing of Self*. Talk for Cornell University on Tuesday, July 20.

[27] This also includes theorising about agential realism itself. Theorising is a material-discursive practice—see text below.

require stories that do justice to how humans, plants, animals, and other earthlings are always already involved in each other lives and make each other possible. The queering (undoing) of identity as nonbinary and gender-fluid applies to humans as well as atoms, neurons, and social amoebas (Barad, 2012a). As model organisms in molecular biology and genetics for studying communication and cell differentiation, slime moulds (*Dictyosteliida*) teach us that it is possible to behave as if you have a brain but don't have one. With a nod to René Descartes, Barad argues that what counts as an individual is not a 'clear and distinct' matter:

> Social amoebas queer the nature of identity, calling into question the individual/group binary. In fact, when it comes to queering identity, the social amoeba enjoys multiple indeterminacies, and has managed to hoodwink scientists' ongoing attempts to nail down its taxonomy, its species-being defying not only classification by phylum but also by kingdom. (Barad, 2012a, p. 27)

Reworking identity as nondualistic and queer "all the way down" has implications for the ontology of theorising (Chap. 3.4) and how we live our lives. Undoing "it" and "self" is not only a human affair: 'the "other" is always already with-in' (Barad, 2019, pp. 43–44). And this includes face masks, SARS-CoV-2, those already dead and those not yet born. Each body, whether human or other-than-human is a quantum entanglement (Sect. 2.2). The diffractive reading of quantum theory through social justice and poststructuralist feminist theories profoundly queers identity, including the 'category of *gay*' (Halberstam, 2020, p. 29). As a relation *within,* and not *without,* a nondual, gender-fluid identity is not an erasure or a flattening of difference. Agential realism troubles conceptions of gender that are based on the ontology of Euclidian mathematics and Newtonian physics: a body is either "this" or "that", "one" or the "other". Instead, agential realism proposes a 'material multiplicity of self': 'diffracted across spaces, times, realities and imaginaries' (Barad, 2014, p. 34).

Barad troubles the very nature of oneness and twoness (the binary type of difference) when diffracting through Gloria Anzaldúa's proposition that 'like other queer people', she (Anzaldúa) is 'two in one body, both male and female' (Barad, 2014, p. 173). Agential realism reworks identity in both space *and* time (Chaps. 1.5 and 1.6). Even binaries such as here/there, now/then, inner/outer, and human/matter are in dynamic entangled relation with one another, neither mutually exclusive nor contradictory (Sect. 2.2). It should come as no surprise that agential realism has also inspired fashion theorists. By bringing to the fore the materiality of discourses about embodiment (Sect. 2.4), clothes 'cannot signify without a body, real or imagined, and that even an unworn garment refers to the materiality of an eventual wearer' (Parkins, 2008, p. 506).

When Karen Barad asks the question, 'How can I be responsible for that which **I** love?' (Sect. 2.1) the 'I' in the question does not have the individual Barad—located in space and moving forward in time—as its referent. Barad cannot be located *in* space and time as a bounded body. They (Barad) are part of and entangled with the universe (Fig. 2.1). Barad is iii[28] and *flashes up* like a star in the night sky (Sect. 2.4).

---

[28] Agential realism embraces a posthumanist notion of the self. It disrupts the use of **I**—a Cartesian, bounded self-referential subject who *has* agency, intentions and exists separately from other bodies

2.4 On Subjectivity

Troubling widely held and deeply engrained notions of the scale of matter, Barad (2017a, p. G109) proposes that

> We are stardust – made of atoms cooked inside of stars through a process of nuclear fusion – all the while, a brilliance "brighter than a thousand suns" resides inside the nucleus of an atom. The largest of space-time-matter measures, the smallest of space-time-matter measures: *each contained inside the other, each threaded through the other. A strange topology.*

Agential realism indeed 'gets inside our skin' and reworks notions of contiguity and (queer)identity (Sect. 2.3), iteratively reconfiguring who and what subjects are (Barad, 2007, p. 466). So what would be involved in "meeting Karen Barad" as the title of this chapter promises? Let's re-turn to one of the quotes this chapter starts with, but this time with different emphases:

> …**we participate in bringing forth the world in its specificity, including ourselves**. We have to meet the universe halfway, to move toward what may come to be **in ways that are accountable for our part in the world's differential becoming**. All real living is meeting. And each meeting matters. (Barad, 2007, p. 353; my emphases)

Each one of us is accountable for 'the worlds' differential becoming' and some more than others.[29] Reworking subjectivity as stardust brings us back to Fig. 2.1 and Karen Barad's Facebook profile. In the chapter *What Flashes Up* (2017b), Barad diffracts through Walter Benjamin's work and proposes that constellations are images of particular material configurations of stars. The 'image is dialectics at a standstill' (Barad, 2017b, p. 34). Introducing the figure of a constellation as de(con)structive methodology (see also Chap. 3.5), Barad comments that knowledge comes only in lightning flashes. In the image, '**what has been** comes together in a flash with the **now** to form a constellation' (Barad, 2017b, p. 34; my emphases). When looking at stars in the night sky, they are not the same distance from me, the observer. Barad presents the following argument to de(con)struct[30] chronological time:

> since the speed of light is a constant, when we look at more distant objects we are looking deeper into the past. For example, when we look at our closest star, the sun, we are seeing the way it looked eight minutes ago—that is, we are watching in the present something that happened in the past. Staring at a constellation, we are witnessing multiple different pasts in the present, some more distant than others. Constellations are then images of a specific array of past events, a configuration of multiple temporalities, "a constellation in being." (Barad, 2017b, p. 34)

(see this chapter). Humans do not *have* but *are* porous bodies. Not things in the world, *in* space and time, but relational phenomena—a spacetimemattering iii is a neologism that articulates a notion of identity that is unbounded.

[29] See Chap. 1.2 for the politics of the use of "we" and "us".

[30] The methodology of de(con)struction is introduced in this 2017 chapter. See also: Chap. 3.6. The methodology has also been used to de(con)struct developmental notions of child development and to, e.g., take age out of play (Haynes & Murris, 2019).

The important point here is that Benjamin's lightning flash is not *between* moments in space but *across* times. When we so-called "go back in time", we don't jump back into the past. Interestingly, Barad's agential realism does not reject linear time; the "lines" are entangled multiplicities. So, what are the implications for subjectivity, for notions of self-identity that are tied up with chronological time and for the memories that intuitively seem to belong to me?

To answer this question, we listen to Karen Barad performing their paper *Undoing the Future: Troubling Time/s and Ecologies of Nothingness: Re-Turning, Re-Membering, and Facing the Incalculable* in New York City. It is July 2018. Available on YouTube,[31] the video transcript records the following comments about time (my emphases):

> the interesting things going back to the
> 99:01
> question of grammar about you know **the**
> 99:05
> **question of simultaneity** because we're
> 99:08
> used to talking about you know something
> 99:11
> like even if it seems far-fetched **being**
> 99:14
> **here and there simultaneously** the
> 99:17
> troubling of time here is such that I
> 99:20
> barely know how to say this to speak it
> 99:23
> because **it's not the different times are**
> 99:25
> **happening simultaneously** in a sense it's
> 99:30
> as if in the hereness of here there's
> 99:34
> yesterday today and tomorrow
> 99:37
> so, **it's coexistence that I don't even**
> 99:41
> **think we have a kind of term for**
> 99:46
> because it's so strange to us to think

[31] https://www.youtube.com/watch?v=bMVkg5UiRog.

99:48

of **moments that are bleeding through one**

99:52

another but not in terms of our own

99:54

lives in terms of our own

99:57

phenomenological experience like I was

100:00

saying in the beginning of my lecture

100:02

I'm here now in you know standing **or and**

100:07

even sitting before you as the kid that

100:10

I was in 1984 when I took a job at

100:13

Barnard as well as being you know this

100:17

older person with totally gray hair

100:20

sitting before you and many other and

100:23

many other things these moments bleed

100:25

bleed through one another in ways that I

100:27

think that we're much more used to but

100:29

what I'm saying

100:30

that **those features of time are not**

100:34

merely subjective experiences that's the

100:36

way the world is experiencing itself too-

Diffracting through Benjamin's notion of 'now-time' (*Jetztzeit*), Barad proposes that in the 'thick-now of the present moment', times bleed through one another as quantum entanglements. Diffractively reading the past through the present in the 'thick-now' reveals the potential for justice—not by pinning hopes on some utopian future, but by rupturing the continuum of time and bringing the energetics of the past into the present and the present into the past (Barad, 2017b, pp. 21–23). An example in Chap. 3 explores in some detail how the methodology of de(con)struction and constellation can work in education research with its core concept of 'thick-now'.

Our notions of self-identity that are tied up with chronological time do indeed require an explosive methodology and much unlearning.

2.5 On Specific Connectivity

As we approach the "end" of this chapter, let's re-turn to a quote from *Meeting the Universe* "earlier" (Sect. 2.1), but with a different emphasis:

> This book is about entanglements. To be entangled is not simply to be intertwined with another, as in the joining of separate entities, but to lack an independent, self-contained existence. Existence is not an individual affair. Individuals do not preexist their interactions; rather, individuals emerge through and as part of their entangled intra-relating. **Which is not to say that emergence happens once and for all, as an event or as a process that takes place according to some external measure of space and of time,** but rather that time and space, like matter and meaning, come into existence, are iteratively reconfigured through each intra-action,[32] thereby making it impossible to differentiate in any absolute sense between creation and renewal, beginning and returning, continuity and discontinuity, here and there, past and future. (Barad, 2007, p. ix; my emphases)

Karen Barad tends to avoid concepts such as "emergence", "events", and "process" —popular concepts (also) in posthumanist and new materialist writing. The problem is that they often assume unilinear time and suggest some kind of containment (they can be "finished").

Footnotes are where significant troubling often takes place in Barad's writings, as in their comment about the standard (mis)reading of Haraway's well-known notion of situatedness (see Footnote 45, Barad, 2007, pp. 470–471):

> Haraway does not take location to be about fixed position (though unfortunately many readers who cite Haraway conflate her notion of "situated" with the specification of one's social location along a set of axes referencing one's identity).

On the contrary, different spaces and temporalities bleed through one another in the "here" and "there" and "past" and "future" in the "thick-now" (Sect. 2.4). For both Haraway and Barad, it is not self-evident that bodies are bounded by their skin. Bodies are not concrete facts *in* the world. They do not 'occupy particular coordinates in space and time, in culture and history' (Barad, 2007, p. 376), because:

> situation is never self-evident, never simply 'concrete,' [but] always critical, " "the kind of standpoint with stakes in showing how 'gender, ' 'race,' or **any structured inequality** in each interlocking specific instance gets built into the world-i.e., not 'gender' or 'race' as attributes or as properties, but 'racialized gender' as a practice that builds worlds and objects in some ways rather than others, **that gets built into objects and practices and exists in no other way**. Bodies in the making, not bodies made. (Barad, 2007, p. 159; my emphases)

---

[32] Intra-action is not only about a change from 'presumed separability to nonseparability (relational ontology) but entails a radically different understanding of causality and an ontoepistemological framework with implications for thinking about questions of justice' (Barad, 2017a, p. G119, ftn 17).

Location might be about specificity, as, for example, an email address is specific on the internet, but *the specificity is not fixed*. Barad continues in the same footnote by diffracting through Haraway. This practice of reading texts diffractively through one another is an affirmative feminist methodology that is not critical but that creates new insights by merging ideas as waves do when they encounter an obstruction in the sea (Chap. 4). This is ontologically very different from a typical literature review, which assumes that you are at an ontological distance from "bodies" of literature, having a bird's eye point of view—creating an overview by comparing, contrasting, juxtaposing, or looking for similarities and themes (Murris & Bozalek, 2019, pp. 1105–1106). Without criticising Haraway, Barad shares the insight produced through the diffraction:

> Though Haraway doesn't seem to go as far in making the ontological points I want to emphasize here, in both accounts it seems that while location cannot be about occupying a fixed position, it may be usefully (con)figured as *specific connectivity*. (Barad, 2007, pp. 470–471, ftn 45)

As so often when reading Barad's work, the *foot*-notes help us *walk around* in concepts.[33] The footnotes are diffracted through the 'main' text, rather than being external to the text. They are not *outside* the text, in the same way that other bodies, such as human bodies, have no outsides. Barad (2019, p. 42) argues that all bodies (micro *and* macro) are unbounded by their skin because each "self" or "individual" is already 'made up of all possible histories of virtual intra-actions with all others'. Inspired by Jacques Derrida, they propose that difference is the ontological starting point for agential realist intra-active relationality (Chap. 1). This is a difference *without identity*, as the latter assumes something outside itself. In the undoing of "it" and "self", the Derridean notion of hospitality is not only a human affair: 'the "other" is always already with-in' (Barad, 2019, pp. 43–44) (Chap. 1.4).

The idea of 'exteriority within phenomena' points at *agential separability*—the key notion, Barad admits,[34] of their 2014 paper *Diffracting Diffraction—Cutting Together Apart*. The spacetime location (*as specific connectivity*) is Santa Cruz and the colleagues who Barad felt were not given sufficient credit for the diffractive methodology:

> thanks to the enormous labours and persistence of women of colour, questions of differences broke through the breakwater of Universal Sisterhood, built on the foundations of sameness and shared commonalities, to become vital to, if not the lifeblood of, feminist theorizing. (Barad, 2014, p. 169)

The reason for writing about diffraction here is that it helps to articulate the notion of what it means to be a response-able colleague and friend. It also helps us to think differently about history, including our "own" (see the cascading question about memory in 2.3). This is explored further in the following chapters through examples from practice. Barad writes:

---

[33] See Chap. 4.1.

[34] About the seminar in Cape Town, see Chap. 1, Footnote 17.

Let's begin by re-turning (to) the past—to a key moment in feminist theorizing about diffraction. Rather than zooming in on one moment in time (as if there were such an infinitesimal temporal slice or instant of time that could be naturally picked out from a presumed whole line of sequential points) in order to see the infinity that lives through it, we re-turn to a thicker 'moment' of spacetimemattering—which we might designate by the spacetime coordinates Santa Cruz, CA late 1980s/early 1990s.

While radiating more than modesty and generosity, yet also including those virtues, the 2014 paper diffracts through passages of texts by Trinh Minh-ha and Gloria Anzaldúa. This performative practice does justice to how new ideas materialise, *because of the specificity of the particular configuration* of people thinking together as well as the ocean that is very much part of the paper too.[35] Surfing on waves, the diffractive "genre" of writing breaks out of the usual ontology and troubles the agentially separate way in which we tend to read "moments" in history:

This moment is dispersed/diffracted throughout the paper, and this moment, like all moments, is itself a diffracted condensation, a threading through of an infinity of moments-places-matterings, a superposition/ entanglement, never closed, never finished. (Barad, 2014, p. 169)

Re-turning[36] to such dispersed/diffracted moments in time requires doing research differently. Again, a "small" earthling is entangled with Barad in their reasoning. This time it is a worm.

We might imagine re-turning as a multiplicity of processes, such as the kinds earthworms revel in while helping to make compost or otherwise being busy at work and at play: turning the soil over and over—ingesting and excreting it, tunnelling through it, burrowing, all means of aerating the soil, allowing oxygen in, opening it up and breathing new life into it. (Barad, 2014, p. 168)

Re-turning as a composting methodology and doing justice to the intricate detail of specific connectivity helps to deal 'with the ravages of performative and technicist policies that are increasingly governing higher education practices' (Leibowitz & Bozalek, 2018, p. 982). This kind of "Slow scholarship" is not necessarily about doing things more slowly, but about the way things are done ethically and politically. In the Acknowledgements of a book in which their chapter is published, Barad graciously thanks the editors for their patience and powerfully articulates how their use of the constellation as methodology made them miss 'innumerable deadlines'[37]:

I found myself taken in by the configurations and felt amazement as each one expanded, shifted and reconstellated again; the project felt like it would burst under this pressure, as it kept expanding in more directions. (Barad, 2017b, p. 76)

Like the Slow Food Movement (Petrini, 2007), where the idea originates from, "Slow" is not just about slowness/speed, but about thinking together differently,

---

[35] Barad tells this in response to a question during a seminar in Cape Town. See Chap. 1 ftn 17.

[36] See also see this Chap. 3.1 for more on "re-turning".

[37] The writing of this chapter was also delayed by the deaths of a good friend and of their father Harold Barad (Barad, 2017b, p. 76).

ethically, aesthetically, ecologically, and with 'a willingness to engage across differences of discipline and ideas' (Leibowitz & Bozalek, 2018, pp. 982–983). Barad's Slowness is of an ontoepistemologicalethical kind—a doing justice (ethics) to the complexity (epistemological) of the world of which we are a part (ontological). In an interview, Barad reiterates how *Meeting the Universe* will always remain 'open':

> For one thing, the book doesn't end (nor did it start) with its publication. Or rather, it's an open book, if I can put it that way; it's temporally open, and it continues to draw my attention back to it. My work continues to be in conversation with it. I'm re-turning, turning it over and over again. Wondering if I could have said something better, if I shouldn't have left out a chapter on Foucault that I decided to cut, if I shouldn't have published the new physics results in physics journals first, what further elaborations weren't included and still await being written up in publishable form and which ones I have ideas about but will probably never have the time to get to. And a major part of that is coming finally back around to the topic of my dissertation: quantum field theory. (Barad in Barad & Gandorfer, 2021, pp. 133–134)

In Chap. 3, we worm our way through an open dispersed/diffracted moment of when a photo of a young person was taken during a research project—re-turning to data from an international project on play with technology. You will meet "six-year" old Zuko and engage in an experimental reading of the image as a constellation: 'dialectics at a standstill' (Barad, 2017b, p. 34). We will trace the photo (Fig. 3.1) as a Baradian phenomenon and explore how measurements are agential performative practices that make worlds (Barad, 2012b, p. 6). iii will re-turn to previous writing and rework the data by tracing different entanglements, paying attention to the intricate details that matter ethically and politically. However, justice is not a state or an endpoint that can be achieved once and for all. We should take it to heart that

> there is only the ongoing practice of being open and alive to each meeting, each intra-action, so that we might use our ability to respond, our responsibility, to help awaken, to breathe life into ever new possibilities for living justly. The world and its possibilities for becoming are remade in each meeting. (Barad, 2007, p. x)

References

Barad, K. (2007). *Meeting the universe halfway: Quantum physics and the entanglement of matter and meaning.* Duke University Press.

Barad, K. (2012a). Nature's queer performativity (the authorized version). *Kvinder, Køn & Forskning/women, Gender and Research, 1–2,* 25–53.

Barad, K. (2012b). What is the measure of nothingness? Infinity, virtuality, justice/Was ist das Maß des Nichts? Unendlichkeit, Virtualität, Gerechtigkeit, dOCUMENTA (13): 100 Notes—100 Thoughts/100 Notizen—100 Gedanken I Book N°099 (English & German edition, 2012).

Barad, K. (2014). Diffracting diffractions: Cutting together-apart. *Parallax, 20*(3), 168–187.

Barad, K. (2015). TransMaterialities: Trans*/matter/realities and queer political imaginings. *GLQ, 21*(2–3), 387–422.

Barad, K. (2017a). No small matter: Mushroom clouds, ecologies of nothingness, and strange topologies of spacetimemattering. In A. Lowenhaupt Tsing, H. A. Swanson, E. Gan, & N. Bubandt

(Eds.), *Arts of living on a damaged planet: Ghosts and monsters of the Anthropocene* (pp. G103–120). University of Minnesota Press.

Barad, K. (2017b). What flashes up: Theological-political-scientific fragments. In C. Keller & M.-J. Rubenstein (Eds.), *Entangled worlds: Religion, science, and new materialisms* (pp. 21–88). Fordham University Press.

Barad, K. (2019). After the end of the world: Entangled nuclear colonialisms, matters of force, and the material force of justice. *Theory & Event, 22*(3), 524–550.

Biagioli, M. (1999). *The science studies reader*. Routledge.

Halberstam, J. (2020). *Wild things: The disorder of desire*. Duke University Press.

Haraway, D. (2016). *Staying with the trouble: Making kin in the Chthulucene*. Duke University Press.

Haynes, J., & Murris, K. (2019). Taking age out of play: Children's animistic philosophising through a picturebook. *The Oxford Literary Review, 41*(2), 290–309. https://doi.org/10.3366/olr.2019.0284

Heijnol, A. (2017). Ladders, trees, complexity, and other metaphors in evolutionary thinking. In A. Tsing, H. Swanson, E. Gans, & N. Bubandt (Eds.), *Arts of living on damaged planet* (pp. G87–103). University of Minnesota Press.

Hohti, R., & Osgood, J. (2020). Pets pets that have 'something inside': The material politics of in/animacy and queer kin within the childhood menagerie. *Geneaology, 4*(2), 38.

Juelskjær, M., Plauborg, H., & Adrian, S. (2021). *Dialogues on agential realism: Engaging in worldings through research practice*. Routledge.

Juelskjær, M., & Schwennesen, N. (2012). Intra-active entanglements: An interview with Karen Barad. *Kvinder, Køn & Forskning, 21*(1–2), 10–23.

Leibowitz, B., & Bozalek, V. (2018). Towards a slow scholarship of teaching and learning in the South. *Teaching in Higher Education, 23*(8), 981–994. https://doi.org/10.1080/13562517.2018.1452730

Mayberry, M. (1998). Reproductive and resistant pedagogies: The comparative roles of collaborative learning and feminist pedagogy in science education. *Journal of Research in Science Teaching: the Official Journal of the National Association for Research in Science Teaching, 35*(4), 443–459.

Murris, K. (2016). The posthuman child: Educational transformation through philosophy with picturebooks. In G. Dahlberg & P. Moss (Eds.), *Contesting early childhood series*. Routledge.

Murris, K. (2019). Choosing a picturebook as provocation in teacher education: The 'posthuman family'. In C. R. Kuby, K. Spector, & J. J. Thiel (Eds.), *Posthumanism and literacy education: Knowing/becoming/doing literacies* (pp. 156–170). Routledge. https://doi.org/10.4324/9781315106083

Murris, K. (2020). Posthuman de/colonising teacher education in South Africa: Animals, anthropomorphism and picturebook art. In P. Burnard & L. Colucci-Gray (Eds.), *Why science and art creativities matter: STEAM (re-)configurings for future-making education* (pp. 52–78). Brill Publishers. https://brill.com/view/title/54614

Murris, K. (2021a). Making kin: Postqualitative, new materialist and critical posthumanist research. In K. Murris (Ed.), *Navigating the postqualitative, new materialist and critical posthumanist terrain across disciplines: An introductory guide* (pp. 1–22). Routledge.

Murris, K. (2021b). The 'missing peoples' of critical posthumanism and new materialism. In K. Murris (Ed.), *Navigating the postqualitative, new materialist and critical posthumanist terrain across disciplines: An introductory guide* (pp. 62–85). Routledge.

Murris, K., & Borcherds, C. (2019a). Body as transformer: 'Teaching without Teaching' in a Teacher Education Course. In C. Taylor & A. Bayley (Eds.), *Posthumanism and higher education: Reimagining pedagogy, practice and research* (pp. 255–277). Palgrave Macmillan. https://doi.org/978-3-030-14672-6_15

Murris, K., & Borcherds, C. (2019b). Childing: A different sense of time. In D. Hodgins (Ed.), *Feminist post-qualitative research for 21st childhoods* (pp. 197–209). Bloomsbury Academic. https://doi.org/10.5040/9781350056602

Barad, K., & Gandorfer, D. (2021). Political desirings: Yearnings for mattering(,) differently. *Theory & Event, 24*(1), 14–66.

Murris, K., & Bozalek, V. (2019). Diffraction and response-able reading of texts: The relational ontologies of Barad and Deleuze. *International Journal of Qualitative Studies in Education, 32*(7), 872–886. https://doi.org/10.1080/09518398.2019.1609122

Murris, K., & Muller, K. (2018). Finding child beyond 'child': A posthuman orientation to foundation phase teacher education in South Africa. In V. Bozalek, R. Braidotti, M. Zembylas, & T. Shefer (Eds.), *Socially just pedagogies: Posthumanist, feminist and materialist perspectives in higher education* (pp. 151–171). Palgrave Macmillan.

Murris, K., Reynolds, R., & Peers, J. (2018). Reggio Emilia inspired philosophical teacher education in the Anthropocene: Posthuman child and the family (tree). *Journal of Childhood Studies: Interdisciplinary Dialogues in Early Childhood Environmental Education Special Issue, 43*(1), 15–29.

Murris, K., & Somerville, M. (2021). Planetary literacies in the Anthropocene. In J. Z. Pandya, R. A. Mora, J. Alford, N. A. Golden, & R. S. De Roock (Eds.), *Routledge handbook of critical literacies*. Routledge.

Nelson, L. H., & Nelson, J. (Eds.). (1997). *Feminism, science and the philosophy of science*. Kluwer.

Parkins, I. (2008). Building a feminist theory of fashion: Karen Barad's Agential Realism. *Australian Feminist Studies, 23*(58), 501–515.

Petrini, C. (2007). *Slow food nation: Why our food should be good, clean, and fair*. Rizzoli Ex Libris

Rouse, J. (2004). Barad's feminist naturalism. *Hypatia, 19*(1), 142–161.

Tsing, A. L. (2015). *The mushroom at the end of the world: On the possibility of life in capitalist ruins*. Princeton University Press.

Chapter 3
Agential Realism and Response-Able Education Science

3.1 Introduction: 'We Are a Part of that Nature We Seek to Understand'

English and Gender Studies scholar Jack Halberstam speaks highly about Karen Barad's influential work on quantum physics and its importance for research in the Humanities. Hollin et al. (2017, p. 919) note that it is striking how Barad's philosophy-physics 'dealing with quantum mechanics, double-slit experiments, wave-particle duality, and Bohrian notions of complementarity has been engaged with so readily across [academic] fields'.[1] Halberstam underscores how we often refer to outdated understandings of science (Newtonian, Einsteinian, etc.). In contrast, Karen Barad offers us: 'a completely different registering of the world through quantum physics' and although it is 'something that is just out of our grasp or reach for many of us', radically different understandings of the human and body and time become possible.[2] Agential realism makes it possible to break with deeply racialised understandings of the body through another grammar and vocabulary. This helps us to understand 'wrong' bodies that are 'out of place' and 'out of time'—'fragmentary internally contradictory bodies' that don't fit normalised humanist discourses about the human.[3] The Baradian point is not simply to include matters of race, gender, sexuality, disability, or age[4] in their reading of quantum physics, but to take seriously

---

[1] Hollin et al. (2017, pp. 919–921) mention the influence of Barad's philosophy-physics on social and natural sciences, science and technology studies, cultural theory, economics, media, social movement studies, theoretical psychology, and even Hegelian philosophy.

[2] See Footnote 1.

[3] From: https://www.youtube.com/watch?v=iHaBEi5a0_0.

[4] Age is not really referred to in posthumanism as a category of exclusion. Children are the "missing peoples" of both humanism and posthumanism. See Murris (2021).

K. Murris, *Karen Barad as Educator*,
SpringerBriefs on Key Thinkers in Education,
https://doi.org/10.1007/978-981-19-0144-7_3

how power is understood in science studies (Barad, 2007, p. 58). Social variables such as age, gender, class and so on, are not properties of individual people. They discursively and materially constitute the subject ontologically. Barad's significant contribution is to see the ontological implications of what quantum physicist Niels Bohr thought were mainly epistemological issues. Despite its profound complexity, and some might say "counterintuitive" implications, quantum theory in research has become more mainstream in the Humanities and Education, although not necessarily how Barad uses quantum physics (Sellberg & Hinton, 2016). Barad reads quantum field theory diffractively through queer theory. As argued in Chap. 1, and re-turned to in this chapter, in a diffractive reading, every researcher is part of the quantum entanglement and part of the apparatus that measures.

Barad takes us on a detailed tour through the history of quantum physics[5] in Chapter seven—a chapter they (Barad) often teasingly refer to in their keynotes as the one that many tend to skip. In Barad's "only"[6] monograph to date, *Meeting the Universe Halfway: Quantum physics and the Entanglement of Matter and Meaning* (2007), we learn in much detail about the contested nature of light as either a particle or wave depending on the configuration of the measuring device. Their diffractive readings of the two-slit experiment and the quantum eraser experiment, offer science across disciplines a profound undoing of identity through the dis/continuity at the heart of matter itself (Sect. 3.8). Key in agential realism is the diffractive methodology (Chap. 4), which is non/representational.

Another way of putting this is that for Barad, there is no "pure" quantum physics.[7] Their reading of physics isn't 'straight', but 'queer' (Juelskjær et al., 2021, p. 13). In the Humanities, Education and Social Sciences the possibility of having different interpretations in academic disciplines is seen as normal and inevitable. Yet, it doesn't imply that Barad's agential realism is subjective and not "real" science. Agential realism is a philosophy about the *real* (empirical[8]) world and is regarded as *objective*. Agential realism reconfigures important concepts in science, such as "subjectivity"[9] and "objectivity". This chapter engages with these key concepts through the detailed agential realist analysis of a photo. This intra-active reading of data is performed through *nonbinary* understandings of "objectivity" entangled with the notion of *response-able* science (Sect. 3.7).

---

[5] For an excellent talk by Karen Barad about the crucial "findings" from quantum physics for agential realism, see: https://www.artandeducation.net/classroom/video/66314/karen-barad-re-membering-the-future-re-con-figuring-the-past-temporality-materiality-and-justice-to-come.

[6] This is another example Barad's Slow scholarship. See Chap. 2 where Barad comments on their "mono"graph as an open book.

[7] For Barad, all scientific practices are 'conceptually, methodologically, and epistemologically allied along particular axes of power' (Barad, 2007, p. 40). For a further articulation of how physics and politics are entangled, also with militarism, colonialism, and racism, see especially Barad's later writing (2017, 2018, 2019).

[8] See Sect. 3.5 for the agential realist reworking of "empirical".

[9] See also (Chap. 2.4).

Let's re-turn[10] to another chapter in *Meeting the Universe Halfway* (2007) to help guide educators through this philosophical maze. In Chap. 1, Barad engages with two scientific orientations that are dominant, also in education science: scientific realism and social constructivism. In their discussion, Barad re-turns to their 1996 chapter entitled *Meeting the Universe Halfway: Realism and Social Constructivism without Contradiction*,[11] but clarified in their 2007 book how the ontology of agential realism isn't like that of social constructivism and why this matters for empirical analysis.

For a scientific realist, science discovers human-independent facts *about* nature (e.g., the nature of children and how they develop). In realist accounts of objects and subjects,[12] nature itself remains untouched by practices of knowing it (e.g., observing children playing doesn't change their play[13]). Scientific realism assumes practices of observing, measuring, and weighing children with a detached (adult) human gaze. It has given birth to the notion of 'child experts': teachers, paediatricians, social workers, psychologists, neuro-scientists, but not children, parents or other members of the community.

For a social constructivist, culture and context are paramount in understanding reality—knowledge jointly developed with other (human) individuals through language and other semiotic systems (e.g., children's play cannot be discovered as something separate from humans making sense of these practices through language).

Barad forcefully articulates the paradigmatic ontologies of each theory and why they are a problem. In important ways, scientific realism and social constructivism have more in common than is obvious at first sight. They both subscribe to *representational* notions of subjects and objects as discrete things (bodies) *in* the world (Chap. 1). In scientific realism, objects are represented as they *really are* (i.e., nature), or, as in social constructionism, the objects are *the product of social activities* (i.e., culture) (Barad, 2007, p. 48). For example, these orientations agree that semiotic systems, such as language, visual images, concepts, audiotapes, etc., *mediate* human access to the material world (Barad, 2007, p. 48).[14] For a social constructivist, science doesn't mirror nature but culture (Barad, 2007, p. 40). But Barad (2007, p. 418) points out the methodological flaw that leave their ontologies untouched: 'Turning the mirror around, as it were, is a bad method for trying to get the mirror in the picture'.

---

[10] For the methodology of re-turning, see especially Chap. 2.5.

[11] Interestingly, the editors of the book in which Barad's chapter was published describe agential realism as a form of social constructivism 'according to which the objects of science are inseparable from the theories and theorizers that posit them', which they say, 'is sufficient to avoid relativism'.

[12] It is important to note that nowadays scholars in science studies (including Barad) are more interested in realism about *entities* than *theories*, that is, in the examination of *experimental practices* (Barad, 2007, p. 41). For example, electrons cannot be "found", yet they are real, because they can *intervene* in causal chains and affect something else (Barad, 2007, p. 41).

[13] A good example of scientific realist "research" is the television series *The Secret Lives of Children* (https://www.channel4.com/programmes/the-secret-life-of-4-and-5-year-olds). See also Michael Rosen's interesting commentary: https://www.radiotimes.com/tv/entertainment/secret-life-of-five-year-olds-channel-4-unethical/.

[14] For an image that might be helpful, see Fig. 4.1 in Murris (2016, p. 87).

For agential realism to make sense, we need to get to the mirror in the picture and "step back" from the *epistemological* issues at hand—the problems about *how humans know something.* We need to *ask prior questions,*[15] for example, 'What is already given ontologically?', and 'What is assumed to be true (a priori) before these scientific practices, informed by these theories, get underway?'. According to Barad (2007, p. 41), these ontological questions haven't been ignored but have not been given enough attention by scientists. Scientific realism and social constructivism draw on the ontologies of Euclidian mathematics and Newtonian physics. They assume the independent existence of objects that move through space (as a container) and forward in (unilinear) time. In terms of their theories of knowledge (epistemologies), these frameworks presuppose an independent and *external* world of subjects and objects known by a researcher *representationally* and cognitively through ideas and concepts *inside* the human mind.[16] Barad (2007, p. 48) comments: 'Representationalism is so deeply entrenched within Western culture that it has taken on a common-sense appeal. It seems inescapable, if not downright natural'. *The mirror is not in the picture.*

In representationalism, the (Cartesian) subject breaks along the line of the knowing subject between "internal" and "external" and 'the asymmetrical faith in word over world'—a distinction as old as Greek philosopher Democritus (Barad, 2007, p. 48).[17] An *actual* (ontological) gap is created between representations and represented, thereby bringing the *philosophical* concept of *"appearance"*[18] into existence. (For example, do we have *real* access to a child in perception or is it only how a child *appears* to me, the researcher?) Acknowledging Rouse for bringing this to their attention, Barad (2007, p. 49) points out that representationalism 'brings to light the asymmetrical faith in word over world that underlines the nature of Cartesian doubt'.

Although these two contrasting theories are sketched here in their extreme formulations, and you will rarely find them held as such by scientists,[19] they highlight the *asymmetrical relations* "between" nature (what is 'awaiting representation') and culture (what represents).[20] It is the role of the (adult) human in knowledge generation that flashes up and how their (implicit) ontologies are entangled with knowledge-making practices. But not only that. The ontology of agential realism enables identification of the hierarchal, exploitative, and extractive practices dependent upon

---

[15] See especially Chap. 4.3.

[16] In contrast, agential realism offers an analytical frame for asking questions about how space, time and entities come into being in their materiality. Space, time and matter do not exist independently, but emerge simultaneously in the shape of 'spacetimemattering' (Barad, 2007, p. 234).

[17] As Barad (2014, p. 168) explains: "the quantum understanding of diffraction troubles the very notion of *dicho-tomy* – cutting into two – as a singular act of absolute differentiation, fracturing this from that, now from then" (Sect. 3.8).

[18] We are not talking about appearance in the sense of how humans look, dress, etc.—how they appear to each other—but the philosophical concept of "appearance"—one of the key concepts in Western philosophy.

[19] See, e.g., the introduction in Nelson and Nelson (1997).

[20] See especially Chaps. 1 and 4 for why this is so important.

representational theories and their claim to truth (or relativism).[21] Subscribing to representationalism is particularly damaging in education. Why is this?

The world researched by educators tends to be a *social* one in which only humans matter, thereby neglecting all other *non*human forces that are *also* at play (Hultman & Lenz Taguchi, 2010, p. 526). In education, many concepts represent nature (read: "immature child") through culture (read: "mature adult"), with the binary between the two as its ontological organising principle. The culture/nature binary has brought into existence the performative practices of facilitating, nurturing, remediating, guiding, instructing, training, disciplining, protecting, medicating, diagnosing, inculcating to mature child (Table 3.1). These symbolic education practices involve adults representing the world to children. Such forms of representationalism are a response to discourses that position the less-human child as lacking the following by "their" nature (essence): responsibility, maturity, trustworthiness, natural goodness, experience, rationality, norms, and values. The culture/nature binary has produced educational interventions that are (so-called) required to intervene in the natural processes that have left child found wanting (Murris, 2016, p. 109; Murris & Reynolds, 2018). However, these concepts are "apparatuses" (Sect. 3.2) that have materialised into particular figurations of child such as "developing child", "ignorant child", "evil child", "innocent child", "egocentric child" and "fragile child" (Table 3.1). (For a genealogy of the Western theoretical influences, see Murris, 2016, pp. 113–120.)

Education researchers implicitly work with these figurations and, as boundary-making practices, they include and exclude, and are therefore always political.[22] They are a form of *slow violence*. Rob Nixon's powerful notion of 'slow violence' plays out across different temporalities. It is a 'violence that occurs gradually and out of sight, a violence of delayed destruction that is dispersed across time and space, an attritional violence that is typically not viewed as violence at all' (Nixon, 2011 in Colebrook, 2020, n.p.). These figurations not only position child as deficit but do their discriminating work in the "thick-now" of the present (Chap. 2.4). Table 3.1 brings the representational mirror in the picture, focusing on adult/child relations and pedagogies.

In my work as a teacher–educator, iii[23] invite student teachers to trace these figurations in the "now" through childhood memories and making transmodal bodymind maps (Murris, 2016, Ch. 5). This de(con)structive work is critical because the normative, (adult) human-made culture/nature binary privileges intelligence of a particular kind over others. This is especially the representational kind that relies on language and abstraction ("a brain on sticks"), which puts the (adult) human at a distance of the world. Barad's observation about rationality is particularly poignant in the context of researching with young children: 'the notion of rational thought as a particular

---

[21] For example, the influence of poststructuralists Judith Butler and Foucault on the development of agential realism is profound, despite its human-centeredness (see Barad, 2007, pp. 34–35 and 145–146). 'Poststructuralism makes evident the politics of the productive nature of social practices and the discursive constitution of the subject' in its radical critique on individualist ontologies (Barad, 2007, p. 410, ftn 12).

[22] See: https://www.youtube.com/watch?v=-LeW-0xN3nQ.

[23] For the use of "iii" instead of "I", see Chap. 1.

Table 3.1 Figurations of child that presuppose representationalism and the culture/nature dichotomy

Culture: adult representational interventions	Nature: what child is "lacking"	Figurations of child	Western philosophies and education theories
Maturation Guidance	Maturity	Developing child	Aristotle, Darwin, Piaget, Vygotsky
Instruction Training	Rationality Experience	Ignorant child	Plato, Aristotle, Locke
Control Discipline Inculcation Drawing in	Trustworthiness Natural goodness	Evil child	Christianity esp. Protestantism
Protection Facilitation	Responsibility	Innocent child	Romantics (Rousseau)
Socialisation Moral guidance Inculcation	Empathy Social norms Moral values	Egocentric child	Piaget Kohlberg
Protection Medication Diagnoses Remediation	Resilience	Fragile child	Psycho-medical scientific model Neuroscience

modality of having well defined concepts, where one foot is put after the next, in order to "think correctly"' (Barad in Barad & Gandorfer, 2021, p. 32).

Barad (2007, pp. 44–45) introduces agential realism as shifting 'the focus from the nature of representations (scientific and other) to the nature of discursive practices (including technoscientific ones)'. The emphasis on discursive practices and their relation to material phenomena enables causal explanations and empirical analyses.[24] Agential realism thereby rejects epistemological relativism; it embraces a particular kind of realism that renders irrelevant the epistemological problems generated by scientific realism and social constructivism (Barad, 2007, pp. 44–45). Humans are not simply gazing passively at the events around them. Instead, they are *part of the world* and even when gazing at the world 'one must actively intervene' (Barad, 2007, p. 51). Unlike representationalism, which positions us above or outside the world, a performative account insists on understanding thinking, observing, and theorising as practices of engagement with, and as part of, the world in which we have our being. Performativity, properly construed, is not an invitation to turn everything (including material bodies) into words. On the contrary, performativity is precisely a contestation of the excessive power granted to language in determining what is real, for example, through definitions. Barad's agential realism is not like a western realism that presupposes the subject/object and, therefore, the culture/nature binary (as, e.g., Pinch, 2011; and see for their response to Pinch, Barad, 2011).

---

[24] In agential realism the concepts "empirical" and "causality" are reconfigured. See Sects. 3.3 and 3.5.

Unlike mainstream traditional physicists, Barad is interested in investigating how laboratory practices produce the objects of their practices and how knowledge discourse-power practices play a constitutive role in producing phenomena (Barad, 2007, pp. 56–57). Attributing these insights to thinkers before them (e.g., Haraway, Kirby, Rouse) in an earlier publication, Barad (2003, p. 828; my emphasis) summarises the agential realist naturalist ontology as follows:

> On an agential realist account of technoscientific practices, the "knower" does not stand in a relation of absolute externality to the natural world being investigated—there is no such exterior observational point.... "We" are not outside observers of the world. Nor are we simply located at particular places in the world; rather, we are part of the world in its ongoing intra-activity. This is a point Niels Bohr tried to get at in his insistence that our epistemology must take account of the fact that **we are a part of that nature we seek to understand**. Unfortunately, however, he cuts short important posthumanist implications of this insight in his ultimately humanist understanding of the "we."[25]

Posthumanist alternatives to scientific realism and social constructivism propose a break with representationalism through 'performative understandings of naturalcultural practices' (Barad, 2007, p. 49). But what do performative practices mean here? Barad warns: 'Not any arbitrary conception of doings or performances qualifies as performative. And humans are not the only ones engaged in performative enactments (which are different from theatrical performances)' (Barad, 2007, p. 49). How does a performative analysis work in education science? What would be involved in understanding education research as a direct material engagement with the world? We meet Zuko to help us explore these critical questions.

3.1.1 Meeting Zuko

Performative agency breaks from representationalism and reworks many of the concepts we tend to take for granted in science, such as "identity", "matter", "discourse", "causality", "phenomenon", "apparatus", and "agency". Agential realism introduces concepts such as "response-ability", "intra-action", "agential separability", and "iterability", enabling a very different kind of science. A brief, but detailed analysis of an example from practice, diffracted through the knots of this chapter, gives a flavour of how this might work in education science and why it matters. Representationalism governs education research. Sociological, psychological, and historical perspectives[26] dominate what constitutes "data" and how it is interpreted. Venturing into "other" disciplines can cause discomfort and uncertainties. Magdalena Górska in an interview verbalises how nervous she was to overlook complexities and 'flatten relations' when adopting agential realism for her doctorate research into the phenomenon of breathing while resisting the more 'obvious' disciplinary lens of psychology and health:

---

[25] For more on the problematic use of "we", see Chap. 1.

[26] See, e.g., the disciplines represented in teacher education programmes: history, sociology, psychology and the much less common philosophy of education.

"Oh my God, I need to understand the physiology of breathing! I need to understand all of the differences between beings that breathe and how they breathe! What about trees, what about soil, what about underwater beings, what about coral reefs, what about seas, and what about the circulation of air around us? What about technology?" So, I went through a time of total chaos where everything was just so exciting but also extremely frustrating and confusing. This frustration was mostly related to **my need to control the project and to contain it somehow.** This is a problem I still struggle with, while at the same time I know how unnecessary and futile it is. (Juelskjær et al., 2021, p. 25)

Without prescriptive guidelines or set methods, and with so many disciplinary "lenses", how do you know you have got it "right" when doing an agential realist analysis? However, the question itself is not the right one if "right" points at *truth* instead of *justice*. Astrid Schrader suggests that oppositional hierarchies—in Zuko's case the adult/child hierarchy and how we understand the difference between adult and child—can't be changed *in* time, when time is conceived as *modalities of the present*. The latter confuses 'change with movement in time' (Juelskjær et al., 2021, p. 49). Inspired by Jacques Derrida, Schrader proposes that as researchers, we need to restructure our relationship to time itself: the past isn't given, closed and fixed, but 'remains before us' (Juelskjær et al., 2021, p. 49).

Diffracting through Deleuze and Guattari (2014, p. xiv):

The question is not: is it true? But: does it work? What new thoughts does it make possible to think? What new emotions does it make possible to feel? What new sensations and perceptions does it open in the body?

Shifting the question, "How do you know you have got an analysis 'right'?" to one of *pragmatics* is important because it moves away from representationalism. In addition, getting an analysis "right" is about how the analysis works. Following Schrader, Derrida, and Barad, *ethics* and *political relevance* are never separate from the analysis. Temporalising the scientific object enables or disables "response-ability" in scientific practices (Sect. 3.7). The way we know Zuko cannot be separated from who, or what, he is ontologically (Juelskjær et al., 2021, p. 46). In other words, transdisciplinarity is a necessary component of agential realist analyses. It complexifies scientific practices to do justice to the complexity of that nature we are part of and that we seek to understand. For example, what counts as ecologically and politically relevant becomes built into scientific practices and opens up a reconfigured "social justice" agenda in education research that is much more than "social". As a transdisciplinary philosophy, agential realism reconfigures the boundaries between the humanities, natural sciences and the social sciences—"undisciplining" the disciplines.

Knitted together through seven "knots",[27] the remainder of this chapter un/folds by reworking key concepts[28] in education science through an experimental agential realist reading of a photograph in its specificity (Fig. 3.1). The image is part of an

---

[27] For a lengthier explanation of the knotty structure of this book, see Chap. 1.5.

[28] For a very helpful resource, see key terms from https://www.artandeducation.net/classroom/video/66314/karen-barad-re-membering-the-future-re-con-figuring-the-past-temporality-materiality-and-justice-to-come.

Fig. 3.1 Zuko holding Lego bricks in a primary school in Cape Town

open-source data set from a large international research project on learning through play with technology in South Africa.[29]

Through a non/linear series of dis/connected knots, six-year-old Zuko holding plastic Lego[30] bricks is read as a Baradian *phenomenon* (Sect. 3.5), not an object. The knots connect theory and practice, sustain relations and forge new ones. For Barad, 'quality in research' involves 'taking into account the specificity of connections and re-membering that in agential realism connections are quantum entanglements' (Juelskjær et al., 2021, p. 144). There is no straight line binding the concepts from beginning to end. This writing style is progressive, troubles linear logic, and disrupts notions of autonomous subjects and objects (including texts). There are no key arguments running from start to finish in straight lines. There are

---

[29] See: Murris, Karin; Ng'ambi, Dick (2020): Children, Technology and Play—Qualitative Data. figshare. Dataset. https://doi.org/10.25375/uct.12017010.v1.

[30] The bricks are referred to as "Lego" to indicate that they are a cheaper imitation of the brand LEGO. Few South Africans and South African schools can afford "real" LEGO.

no explanations or definitions. There are only key concepts to practice education science. These are reworked through the performative practice of the diffractive reading of "this" photo in its specificity.

In agential realist research, experimentation with writing styles is actively encouraged. It helps un/learn the outdated understandings of science Jack Halberstam referred to at the start of this chapter. Non/representational research legitimises adopting different writing styles (e.g., diffractive), genres (e.g., poetry, dance), grammar (e.g., iii), or the use of unusual other-than-human characters (e.g., Chap. 4.1). In the last case, the aim is not to draw analogies or comparisons between humans and say herons, stingrays or brittlestars, but to trouble human exceptionalism and the binaries the dichotomy brings forth, such as culture/nature, intelligent/stupid, complex/simple, macro/micro (Murris et al., 2021). Different material entanglements produce different unpredictable questions that aim to examine closely the role human concepts, human observers, and human knowledge practices play in doing science (Barad, 2007, p. 248). Agential realism breaks with tradition in science studies to reflect on the subject from the outside. Barad (2007, p. 248; italics in the original) elaborates: '*I engage in the practice of science while addressing entangled questions about the nature of scientific practice*':

> What I didn't grasp initially was how to take **my commitments to response-ability** to **some deeper level** into the very practice of doing of physics and engaging with it, while at the same time knowing that this was necessary. It was something that preoccupied me from the start. (Barad in interview Juelskjær et al., 2021, p. 119; my emphasis)

and

> So, I want to understand the ways in which **certain forms of violence** are written into the practices of knowledge and world-making and even into the very equations about matter and nothingness and the nature of the universe. (Barad in interview Juelskjær et al., 2021, p. 125; my emphasis)

Inspired by Barad's engagement with quantum physics, my commitment to response-able education science at 'some deeper level' involves an agential realist tracing of the photo in Fig. 3.1, thereby reconfiguring my research as a worlding practice. I also need to pay attention to the 'forms of violence' written into the concepts we routinely use in education. I turn (briefly) to Donna Haraway. Her comments about technoscience are directly relevant for analysing the photo "of" Zuko and profoundly challenge the scientific realist objectivist 'view from nowhere':

> There is no unmediated photograph or passive camera obscura in scientific accounts of bodies and machines; there are only highly specific visual possibilities, each with a wonderfully detailed, active, partial way of organizing worlds .... Understanding how these visual systems work, technically, socially, and psychically, ought to be a way of embodying feminist objectivity. (Haraway, 1988, p. 583)

Agential realism gives us a technology of embodiment (Barad, 1996). Intricately connected to the notion of objective knowledge, the materiality of the body always implies a view from somewhere.[31] Processes of materialisation incorporate material-discursive factors (including gender, race, sexuality, religion, and nationality, as well as class) but also technoscientific and natural factors. Also, what constitutes the "natural" or the "cultural" is part of the investigation. This is because these notions are always already implied in the reconfiguration of the material relations of the world (see Table 3.1).

Experimentation with tracing the photo's intra-active entanglements crystallises the difference that agential realism as a philosophy makes for education science—difference of a scientific, ethical, and (geo)political kind. This will become clear(er) as the chapter un/folds, and the knots weave their intra-active knotted patterns.

Zuko is one of ten "case-study" children in a report published by an international team (Marsh et al., 2020, p. 57) . iii was Principal Investigator (PI) for the South African part of this project, *Children, Technology and Play* (CTAP) in the project's report the experience is structured in terms of individualised subjects and objects in relation. Each subject (mother, father, child) is described according to hegemonic *normative* discourses about age, race, gender, class, ability, place, well-being, and nationality as follows:

> Carla (40) and Alex (44) and their son Zuko (6) live in a modern, bright and spacious house in Pinelands, Cape Town. Carla and Alex are White South Africans. Zuko is Black South African and was adopted when he was a baby. Both of Zuko's parents are self-employed. Carla holds a master's in Clinical Social Work and Alex has as a Bachelor of Arts degree but currently works as a software development manager. Carla is legally blind (she only has 20% of her vision) and has a hearing difficulty. Carla and Alex each have their own home office and use their own laptops, as well as a bigger monitor. They both have iPhones, and the family has an iPad. In Alex's office at home, he has a camera and a GoPro. Zuko has his own camera and a radio in his bedroom which he uses every day. Zuko uses the family's iPad to play virtual games and to listen to audio and video stories. He also uses his parents' smartphones to listen to music and enter numbers on the calculator until the screen is completely filled. At times, Zuko listens to playlists on iTunes which Alex creates based on Zuko's song requests. Alex remarked on Zuko's song choices being mainly rock hits from the 1980s. Zuko watches Apple TV programmes like National Geographic, football and PJ Masks. Music is an essential part of Zuko's life. He considers darkness and silence scary and cannot sleep unless there's some music or sound in the room at night. He loves comic books, and the family consider read-along CDs as an excellent form of technology that gives him more independence when parents cannot read to him.

The human-centred description focuses on Zuko, his fears, his Mum and Dad, their ages, their work, their qualifications, the technology in their possession, how they use it, their likes, dislikes, norms, values, and his Mum's disability. Because this education research project focuses on investigating children's learning through technology, the description homes in on the technology. Interestingly, "we"—adult humans—bring objects into existence through human vision: we "see" an iPad, camera, radio, Apple TV, and so on. However, data from the home visits show a different (additional) understanding Zuko himself brings to technology. For him, materially manipulating

---

[31] See the discussion in Chap. 2.5 of how Haraway's notion of situated knowledges has been misunderstood in the literature.

light switches and batteries is also "about" learning through technology. Indeed, "we" adult humans can learn much from young children's regular (but often unnoticed) disruption of binary logic (see also Chap. 4). Getting to know the image (Fig. 3.1) is an intra-active matter of engagement and not just reserved for the (adult) human.

Barad's philosophy-physics disrupts all (adult) human-made binaries that shape how we think, feel and act: inside/outside, culture/nature, mind/body, objective/subjective, individual/community, cognition/emotions, professional/personal, teaching/learning, and so on. We re-turn to these at the end of this chapter in the light of our intra-active analysis of Fig. 3.1 and pick up some de(con)structing threads. Although this kind of Slow scholarship (Chap. 2.5) might feel overwhelmingly complex and alien, chewing and munching our way through the image in Fig. 3.1—like the hungry caterpillar in Eric Carle's picturebook, *The Very Hungry Caterpillar* (1969),—might help. Not all of it will be digestible, but more so after re-turning to it more than once. Re-turning as a composting methodology[32] does justice to the intricate detail of specific connectivity and different temporalities, in this case, the open dispersed/diffracted "thick-now" (Chap. 2.4) of when a photo "of" Zuko was taken.

3.2 On Apparatus

Even those committed to the poststructuralist dismantling of the humanist subject find it extremely difficult to 'escape the "I"' (St. Pierre, 2011, p. 620). The challenge when analysing Zuko's photo (Fig. 3.1), is to "get to the mirror" (Sect. 3.1)—to become aware of the (adult) "I" who does the representing—to engage fully with the material features of the discursive (MacLure, 2013). Most scientists often don't realise how practices of representing are in and by themselves *performative* and don't simply model. The "represented" and the "representer" already participate in the entangled material-discursive process of their own representation. 'Representationalism would have us focus on what seems to be evidently given, hiding the very practices that produce the illusion of givenness' (Barad, 2007, p. 360). In the case of Fig. 3.1, this is how the technology masks its mediatory role as apparatus.

Typical apparatuses in education research are the instruments used to "collect" data: surveys, interviews, observations, measuring scales, and focus groups. A critical concept here is "data". As with any concept, agential realism invites us to ask what notions of being and time are assumed in the concept of "data". Data are always a material-discursive intra-active[33] production of data/empirical material and emerge as specific entanglements, "agential cuts" (Sect. 3.8). Agential realism troubles the idea that a research design is a politically neutral apparatus that helps observe, record,

---

[32] See Chap. 2.5 and Table 4.1.

[33] Intra-action (as opposed to the familiar 'interaction') is a Baradian neologism that expresses an ontology whereby relationships don't assume the prior existence of independent 'things' that have independent self-contained existence (Barad, 2007).

and measure *what is happening* in a "research site" objectively. It assists in the *interpretation* of data "intersubjectively" (as social constructivists would agree). Posthumanist analysis also disrupts the idea that technology serves as evidence of what *took place* in space and time to answer *in the present* the research questions that were formulated from the outset (Murris & Menning, 2019). Continuously asking questions about justice (not truth) by investigating who and what benefits from the specificity of the agential cuts of the research is an intricate part of doing agential realist research (Juelskjær et al., 2021). The ethical, ontological, and epistemological are intricately connected in agential realism.

When observing Zuko during a home visit in a Cape Town suburb, a researcher—let's call her Zara—uses her iPhone to take photos "of" Zuko. Then, with his Lego-bricks-camera, Zuko takes a photo of Zara as she takes a photo of him. The researcher writes about the powerful image in Fig. 3.1 in her field notes.[34] It soon becomes the icon of the *Children, Technology and Play* (CTAP) project in South Africa.[35] Complex ethical and geopolitical discourses in their materiality are entangled with Zara's choice. The photo shows enough of Zuko's face to make clear it is a young "black" human. Unlike most research on digital play, the project took place in the Global South (2019–2020)—the first project of this kind and scale in South Africa (Marsh et al., 2020). The image articulates this in a flash. The material presence of the Lego[36] bricks enables Zuko's identity to remain confidential, although permission from parents and child (not the bricks) was granted. The image soon took hold as a striking *representation* of the project and has been used for conference presentations, leaflets, and posters to bring the project to a larger audience.[37]

The use of technology was an intricate part of the CTAP project. Young and older researchers used smartphones, wearable cameras, and dictaphones to co-create data. Indeed, digital technologies are a "normal" part of education research. They are so normalised that it is easy to miss the role of *matter* as part of the intra-active entanglement in Fig. 3.1. We learn from and with Barad that matter is agential in the sense of 'bringing forth new worlds' by 'engaging in an ongoing reconfiguring *of* the world' (Barad, 2007, p. 170). In other words, the iPhone and the photo itself (always more than "itself") are an integral 'part' of the world and dynamically reconfigure what *is* (Barad, 2007, p. 170). Apparatuses do not preexist as individual entities and can, but might not, include both humans and other-than-humans (Barad, 2007, p. 434, ftn 65). Apparatuses themselves are phenomena (Sect. 3.5), not just things or objects, and are constituted through particular—not just human—nature culture practices. Crucially, the specific image that the iPhone as apparatus takes is not an *arbitrary* construction of Zara's choices, intentions, ideas, desires, assumptions, etc. (see Barad, 2007, pp. 170–171). Researchers are not "outside" observers of apparatuses. The agential realist analysis doesn't erase Zuko or Zara. On the contrary,

---

[34] This is a good example of an agential cut, a 'cutting-together-apart' (Sect. 3.8).

[35] See: http://etilab.uct.ac.za/lego/.

[36] They are an imitation of the bricks manufactured by the LEGO brand, hence its spelling in lower case. See Footnote 30.

[37] See Footnote 35.

acknowledging the role of research practices in materialisation is an intricate part of doing response-able science (Sect. 3.7). It also raises interesting questions about what it means to decentre the human in agential realist research (Sect. 3.5).

3.3 On Causality

Humans *do* have a role to play in the agential realist analysis of Fig. 3.1. Still, we need to ask ourselves *what is already ontologically given* in the particular part the human has assigned itself in its specificity (see also Sect. 3.2). One example is the general assumption that research design is an effect of our human will and intention. Generously acknowledging Joseph Rouse's influence on their ideas about causality, Barad cites him as follows:

> Most philosophical discussions of causality take the boundaries of causally interacting systems (objects or events) to be already determinate, without asking how such determination occurs… **Intentional interpretation itself is an example of material intra-action on my account**… (Rouse [2000] quoted in Barad, 2007, p. 434, ftn 64; my emphasis)

For an agential realist, boundaries are produced and never fixed, and this includes human intention as a boundary-making practice. What is needed, Barad writes, is 'a method attuned to the entanglement of the apparatuses of bodily production, one that enables genealogical analyses of how boundaries are produced rather than presuming sets of well-worn binaries in advance' (Barad, 2007, pp. 29–30). One of these 'well-worn binaries' in education research is that of adult/child—surprisingly, a binary Barad does not talk or write about, even though the binary exists only because of the culture/nature binary (Sect. 3.1.1). Assigned to the realm of nature, child is found wanting by culture (Murris, 2016, 2021). This is particularly relevant in the analysis of Fig. 3.1. In an interview, Barad elaborates on how the dynamism of indeterminacy and intra-active agency is at the heart of the agential realist reworking of causality (Barad & Gandorfer, 2021, pp. 59–60).

…intra-actively entangled with/in the photo phenomenon are the apparatuses that measure Zuko's progress in becoming more independent, active and agential in learning through play (see e.g., the scale of the deductive research report, Marsh et al., 2020). For example, Zuko's ability to use the Lego bricks symbolically as a camera and turning the gaze around, from researched to researcher, could be interpreted as him taking on a more mature adult role in terms of abstract reasoning.

… intra-actively entangled with/in the photo phenomenon are research ethics discourses and the guidelines followed by both universities involved in Cape Town and Sheffield and the permissions granted by all human research participants. These human-centred discourses foreground the child and put "the rest" into "the background": atmosphere, the room, the weather; the camera pointing at Zuko; the technology of sharing the image via Whatsapp with fellow researchers; the internet and an infinite topological manifold of relata.

… intra-actively entangled with/in the photo phenomenon is Zuko's identity as a "black" six-year-old growing up as an adopted child with white parents in the Cape Town suburb of inelands. His identity matters, but as Barad (2007, p. 246) argues, '[t]he topological dynamics of space, time and matter' are an agential matter but not in a "straightforward" unilinear cause and effect sense.

Tracing entanglements with/in the photo phenomenon is iterative and infinite, yet some tracings matter more than others…

3.4 On Agency

In many ways, the "normal" way of interpreting Fig. 3.1 may seem uncontroversial. As a sign of something else outside itself (MacLure, 2013, p. 663), a socio-cultural scientist might bring Zuko's action and the way he puts the Lego bricks together into the 'scheme of representation'. The photo can be regarded not only as *a* child holding a camera but *more precisely* as a sign of Zuko's agency in symbolising *the camera function* of the iPhone, thereby displaying complex higher-order thinking skills. Zuko is the child-human with agency who "gives" the matter (plastic bricks) symbolic meaning—after all "normally" speaking, matter is mute, passive, immutable, and inert (Barad, 2007, p. 133). In other words, human exceptionalism is written into the grammar of human language. The young human is the creator of a camera that is not real, but *represents* a real camera. Language has been *substantialising*, making the Subject (Zuko) a substance with an essence. The subject-predicate structure of language, "Zuko has agency", reflects an ontology: there is an independently existing child who "has" competencies or attributes. In this sense, language and discourse have positioned us, human animals, as thinkers above or outside the (material) world, and with that same abstractive move have distanced us, 'fully-human' adults, from both matter *and* child (and other so-called "illiterates").

The following comment by Maggie MacLure (2013, p. 663) resonates in analyses such as these:

> Children's actions and affects are fixed and tagged as instances of something else – such as 'behaviour'. But these moments also frustrate the workings of representation and expose the limits of rationality's reductive explanations.

For Barad, agencies do not exist outside phenomena. A material-discursive analysis puts the object, or matter, within the range of analysis by doing justice to the mutually agentic role of matter. Zuko, the bricks, the iPhone, concepts, curriculum documents, apparatuses, research questions, funding agencies, teacher, pedagogies, parents are not just subjects or objects but are all intra-actively entangled and mutually performative transindividual agents. A transindividual analysis resists the sole focus on Zuko's symbolising capacity (e.g., language), his identity (e.g., his race), his origin (e.g., DNA), and intentional action to assess "his" behaviour and learning.

Getting to know the image (Fig. 3.1) is a matter of intra-action and not just reserved for the (adult) human. Theorising is also a material agentic practice—not a representational process *about* the world that takes place *inside* an individual human mind, but 'theorizing is a matter of already engaging as part *of* the world (not even *with* the world)' (Barad in Barad & Gandorfer, 2021, p. 16). Theorising is not only assigned to humans. Theories are 'living and breathing reconfigurings of the world' (Barad, 2012, p. 208). The brittlestar articulates this beautifully with 'superior ingenuity' (Barad, 2014, p. 225) by shedding a limb when in danger from a predator. In doing so, this brainless creature continuously reworks its bodily boundaries (Barad, 2007, p. 375). The spacetime manifold does not sit still while bodies are made and remade. The relationship between space, time, and matter: plastic bricks, metal iPhone, Zuko's body, the land, etc., is much more intimate (Barad, 2007, p. 376). Even the human mind—its so-called uniqueness and its identity—is at stake in agential realism, and so is the nature of matter. The point about the materiality of thinking is not that matter is the condition for a process that itself is not material and simply makes it possible. 'Matter', argues Barad (2015, p. 387), 'is promiscuous and inventive in its agential wanderings: one might even dare say, imaginative':

> Like lightning…involving electrical potential buildup and flows of charged particles: neurons transmitting electrochemical signals across synaptic gaps and through ion channels that spark awareness in our brains. (Barad, 2015, pp. 387–388)

It is matter itself that has 'agential capacities for imaginative, desiring, and affectively charged forms of bodily engagements' (Barad, 2015, p. 387). When reading Fig. 3.1 we need to consider the specificity of the connections in/with/through the photo in all its materiality. How does the material world intra-act with Zuko other than through language? The eye of the iPhone is "silent" about Zuko's heartbeat, his hungry tummy, the urgent need to go to the toilet or his excitement about Zara's visit. The human eye might not be silent when scanning the image, but its register is at a human scale. Nevertheless, these relata are all part of the intra-dependent agency, the dynamically diffracting forces that include affect. "Normal" data "collection" is minimal compared to agential realist performative practices that involve a differential co-articulation of human and nonhuman agencies. The challenge (and opportunity) is to be 'acutely sensitive to details' because 'small differences matter enormously' (Barad in interview with Juelskjær & Schwennesen, 2012, p. 13) and, in our analyses, to do justice to the complexity of the world. '*Agency is a matter of changing the possibilities for change in their materiality*' (Barad & Gandorfer, 2021, p. 59).

3.5   On Phenomenon

In response to a longstanding debate in Western philosophy,[38] Barad takes up the position that 'reality is composed not of things-in-themselves or things-behind-phenomena but of things-in-phenomena' (Barad, 2007, pp. 392–393). In *Meeting the Universe Halfway* (2007, pp. 333–335), Barad elaborates on how Niels Bohr's

---

[38] See the noumena-phenomena debate in Barad (2007, p. 375).

epistemological understanding of *phenomena as the primary units of existence* is the basis for a new ontology 'in a posthumanist direction that decenters the human'.[39] Responding to questions from the audience after a published talk,[40] Barad comments on their use of 'empirical' in scientific analysis:

> the notion that background assumptions are absolutely necessary in both identifying evidence and making any kind of reasoning about evidence is absolutely crucial…what Niels Bohr …gives us is not that he's getting rid of empiricism he's saying what is **the objective referent for any kind of empirical values or data and that is the phenomenon rather than the object itself**. And now we're in a whole other ballgame. Once it's the phenomenon - the material-discursive phenomenon which is **inseparable from the apparatuses that help produce it - we're always already in the realm of before even the split between nature and culture or science and society** and so on and so forth so thanks for the questions.

Barad does not avoid the use of "empirical" in research but reconfigure its meaning. In their answer to the questioner, Barad brings to the fore a vital insight into how *binaries are always already at play* in any empirical analysis: culture/nature, science/society, but also language/matter. Agential realists move in their 'empirical' analyses from describing subjects and objects in their specificity to describing phenomena. So how does this work, and what difference does it make epistemologically, ethically, and politically? Why does Barad suggest this is 'a whole other ballgame' (quote above)?

Let's consider first what it would be like to do a representational reading of Fig. 3.1. Zuko is holding plastic bricks in his hands—playfully and competently arranged *as* a camera. Even before the 'empirical' analysis of Fig. 3.1 gets underway, Zuko is already configured as *a* 'child', a young human being, who is still developing into a more mature human being and responsible citizen, which will come with age. Representational readings come more "naturally", because of the subject-object relationality and the object ontology we have been educated into, making intra-active relationality "counter-intuitive". Human meaning-making (discourses) trumps starting with the material in data analysis, or what even counts as "data". But phenomena are material-discursive, and the hyphen between material and discursive indicates that 'no priority is given to either materiality or discursivity; neither one stands outside the other' (Barad, 2007, p. 177). In a representational reading of the image, we don't "see" the differently coloured plastic bricks covering Zuko's face as such, although of course this could (also) be possible. We, (adult) humans "see" the plastic in the service of the young human who is playing be(com)ing researcher. The bricks *matter* only when the material arrangement in its particularity helps understand children's intentions. For example, psychologists might hypothesise that Zuko is embarrassed and is hiding his face. Although in the sociology of childhood, ascribing particular intentions to children's behaviour in data analysis is discouraged

---

[39] However, not the human is the primary ontological unit, but the phenomenon. See Sect. 3.5.

[40] This is a slightly edited transcription of the video (my emphases), available from https://www.youtube.com/watch?v=bMVkg5UiRog. Karen Barad. *Undoing the Future: Troubling Time/s and Ecologies of Nothingness: Re-Turning, Re-Membering, and Facing the Incalculable*. July 2018.

without children themselves as co-researchers, their analysis would also be human-centred and representational (see Sect. 3.1). In contrast, agential realist analyses are 'anti-anthropocentric', but 'anthropo-situated'.[41]

Zuko *matters* and isn't erased, but *when analysed as a phenomenon,* other stories can be told that trouble power-producing binaries. Moving away from dominant stories such as psychological, sociological, and anthropological ones in education analysis flashes up fresh opportunities to de(con)struct (Sect. 3.6). Plastic bricks are not only toys. They are also materialised (e.g., economic) practices, gendered (Osgood, 2019), and 'congealed labor' (Barad in Juelskjær et al., 2021, p. 138). It is critical to pay attention to the material (labour) conditions in, for example, the factories where the bricks were produced.

The distinction between micro and macro is human-made[42] before the analysis starts or what counts as "empirical". When reading Fig. 3.1 as a phenomenon, it is ontologically the case that Zuko's skin is an assemblage of 'subatomic particles' (Barad, 2007, p. 354) touching the bricks. Made of hard plastic, bright colours, and with its distinct smell, the bricks are also an assemblage of 'subatomic particles'. This kind of touching troubles notions of temporal and spatial scale itself (Barad, 2007). However, binary opposites are social constructions that do not correspond to any actual existing polarities. At the same time, they are 'apparatuses' (Barad, 2007) that profoundly shape research practices. Yet, the issue is not about going *beyond* binaries but about questioning what differentially constitutes these binaries. What are the material and discursive conditions of their production? How do they work to include and exclude, and why does that matter?

Agential realist stories attend to the fine details of the phenomenon, avoiding the use of analogies, comparisons, metaphors, or representations, but without setting up binaries between their alternatives (Chap. 4.1). The trouble with such linguistic and rhetorical devices is that they hide the ontologies of separateness that make their very practices possible. Another way of putting this is that agential realist analyses are *stories,* but not in the usual sense of narration. A "thing" is a story. An "object" is a story. "A child" is a story. So, what kind of narrating are agential realists committed to?

Familiar with the LEGO brand of interlocking plastic brick construction sets, the stories we tell need to disrupt the human/material binary and other power-producing binaries, such as adult/child and work/play. Even the possible suggestion that it is a "playful" construction of the bricks (as a camera), rather than "serious" (adult) work, already uses the work/play binary as its meaning-making apparatus (Sect. 3.2). The concept "toy" does some power-full work to position child as wanting, to help them grow up in the mirror image of their older, more mature humans (so the developmental story goes). By closely examining the role human concepts, human observers,

---

[41] See the discussion about Barad's diffraction through Haraway's influential notion of "situated knowledges" in Chap. 1.5.

[42] Barad doesn't claim that scale doesn't matter, but it simply isn't given: 'There is no scale at which the laws of physics change from quantum physics to Newtonian physics, from "microworld" to "macroworld"; to the best of our knowledge, quantum physics holds at all scales' (Barad, 2017, p. G118, ftn 10).

and human knowledge practices play in practicing science, agential realism inspires more just research practices (Barad, 2007, p. 248). For example, we should treat the meaning of concepts such as "child" and "toy", not as "givens" (e.g., through definitions), but as concepts, worth "walking around in for a while" and see what kind of questions this might generate (Barad & Gandorfer, 2021). This de(con)structive work even helps to "take age out of play" (see Haynes & Murris, 2019). As a concept primarily used in the context of children, toys are often specifically manufactured by adults to assist young children's maturation process into adulthood by representing adult human practices and forms of life. Originally made from natural materials such as twigs, clay, stone, wax and wood, many modern toys are made of plastic, requiring different kinds of relationalities and attachments that have to be learned (e.g., cuddling a plastic teddybear[43]). Since the nineteenth century, toys have had explicit educational purposes.[44]

Phenomena are ontological entanglements. The relata: the photo, the iPhone taking the photo, the plastic bricks, Zuko, the apparatuses that measure, the land are always already entangled in less-than,[45] more-than, and other-than-human relations. But participation in these existing relational networks is uneven.

3.6 On De(con)struction

Analysing data diffractively involves installing oneself in an event of 'becoming-with' the data (Haraway, 2008, p. 16). It does not involve *uncovering* the (symbolic) meaning *behind* the photograph (Fig. 3.1) in a representational way but includes reading the visual other-than-human-body as a phenomenon (Sect. 3.5). Iteratively re-turning to Fig. 3.1, the following description resonates: It is 'one of those life moments when the amorphous jumble of history seems to crystallize in a single instant' (Barad, 2017, p. 39). Reading the image involves considering as many of the infinite elements that are dispersed as multiplicities in spacetime—always already entangled with the photograph. This was discussed in the con/text of Fig. 2.1 in Chapter two—the image of a constellation. In the 'now', time is diffracted through itself: past, present, and future enfold through one another in a nonunilinear manner (Barad, 2010, 2017). As an agential realist reading of the image of Zuko holding the Lego bricks, this chapter diffracts Figs. 2.1 and 3.1 through one another.

Analysing Zuko's photo is *a separate event* from what happened during the home visit. Transcripts and still or moving images do not enable researchers to go back in (unilinear) time and analyse what was "really going on" in or with the child.

---

[43] This was brought to my attention during the Kaleidoscope exhibition in Tampere, Finland in October 2021 as part of the Spinning the Sticky Threads of Childhood Memories conference.

[44] Of course, some educational philosophies explicitly encourage the use of "natural" materials. See e.g., Waldorf education based on the philosophies of Rudolph Steiner.

[45] The normative and political concept of human has positioned some humans as inferior based on age, race, gender, ability, class and so forth.

They are "new"[46] material-discursive events: "crystallised amorphous jumbles of history". The past isn't closed. Each re-turning is different. Moreover, such iterative and diffractive engagement with 'the' data involves not only cognition, but also a be(com)ing affected by the experiences of bodies in relation. This cannot be contained, is not always articulable, nor expressible, and may even be beyond words. My fascination with/in the image grows with each meeting; with each re-turning new questions cascade.

De(con)struction is a powerful methodology in the core binaries that shape current education research practices. Walter Benjamin holds that destruction is a condition of the possibility of construction, hence the spelling of "de(con)struction". In the breakup of the continuum of history as a political act, 'what flashes up' crystallises, and is 'a material de(con)struction of the continuum of history' (Barad, 2017, p. 23). The radical political potential lies in thinking about time anew—diffracting the past through the present moment, like the play of light inside a crystal. One example of this is how the land ...was itself appropriated by adult humans and taken away from the sheep... diffracting the land on which the photo was taken which was itself appropriated by adult humans from the sheep, cattle, elephants, wolves, lions, tigers, wildebeest, and zebras that used to roam the wetlands of the Western Cape (Murris & Crowther, 2018). The imported "alien" pine trees in this suburb outside Cape Town discipline the harsh sea winds from blowing away large volumes of dust from mobile sands. The historicity of the place is entangled with the "thick-now" of the moment the photo was taken. Even if the human body doesn't register it, it is still "there". St Pierre (2011, p. 618) reminds us that deconstruction for Jacques Derrida is not just about language, but about 'paying attention to the material structure we call the *human being*' and the '*principle of individuation*' that human-centredness brings with it.

3.7   On Response-Ability

In response-able science, not only Zuko, but also the Lego bricks and the photo itself are liberated from their so-called passive, inert dumbness. These analyses articulate their stories and allow them to respond. Astrid Schrader suggests that response-ability is about the 'enabling of responsiveness within experimental relatings', in other words, maintaining in the analysis throughout and with/in each re-turning Zuko's ability to respond to experimental probings. The notion of response-ability involves paying re-newed attention to research design, to questions asked during home visits, and providing certain technologies to measure play (e.g., wearable cameras), etc.

The photo, Zuko, the plastic bricks are not analysed as individually existing concrete objects/subjects with/in the world (e.g., as part of a causal chain of events), but as already in relation. The relation, not the thing, is ontologically prior. This co-emergence of matter and meaning in the making of the world produces more

---

[46] Agential realism troubles the new/old binary, as every iteration leaves traces and marks on bodies.

complex understandings and expressions of reality that include historicity and the political.

Barad's agential realism reworks objectivity as agential responsibility, and agency as embodied, worldly, and intra-active (Rouse, 2004). Education sciences and schooling continue to place objectivity in high esteem and as central to notions such as quality, rigour, and accountability. However, the kind of objectivity Barad is interested in, avoids binary logic and so does not assume the objective/subjective binary (with intersubjectivity as an intermediate position) (Barad, 2017, p. 37). Although it might be a *matter of fact* that Zuko is taking the initiative and enjoys the play activity that was the measuring scale designed by adult humans at the LEGO Foundation[47] and used as an apparatus. Humans are neither detached observers *of* the world nor located at particular points *in* the world. They 'are part of the world in its ongoing intra-activity' (Barad, 2007, p. 184). Barad takes up the challenge head-on when they ask 'Is it possible to secure objectivity on ontological, rather than merely epistemological, grounds?' (Barad, 2007, p. 331).

Objectivity is not just about how we *know* the world, for example, by interpreting or discovering why Zuko is holding the Lego bricks in *this particular way*, pointing them at the researcher (Fig. 3.1). One of the most compelling insights from the most challenging chapter in *Meeting the Universe Halfway* is that measurements are physical processes. Barad thereby manages to honour Bohr's profound insights concerning the relationship between concepts and physical arrangements without re-inserting the human into their agential realism (Barad, 2007, p. 331). Agential realism says something meaningful about the physical world, about reality. A Baradian notion of objectivity does not nihilate subjectivity (Zara who took the photo) or erase the subject (Zuko). It does not regard objectivity as achieved by disentangling and disengaging the subject from the object (as in much research). It achieves it by taking responsibility for how the knowing subject (me and you, the reader) and her apparatuses (e.g., digital technology) are always already ontologically entangled in what is produced (Barad, 2007). This position is intriguingly phrased as: 'Subjectivity and objectivity are not opposed to one another; objectivity is not subjectivity' (Barad, 2014, p. 175).

At the very time, when is objectivity in researching Zuko and the plastic bricks ethical and political—a matter of response-ability? Objectivity is simultaneously an epistemological, ontological, aesthetic, and ethical issue. Scientific practices and questions of responsibility and accountability cannot be disentangled. As researchers, we are 'accountable for *marks on bodies*, that is, specific materializations in their differential mattering' (Barad, 2007, p. 178; my italics). We are responsible for the cuts that we help enact, not because we do the choosing (neither do we escape responsibility because "we" are "chosen" by them), but because we are an agential part of the material be(com)ing of the universe.

---

[47] For the rubric that measures learning through play, see: https://www.legofoundation.com/media/ 2884/an-introduction-to-the-learning-through-play-experience-tool-zooming-in-on-the-five-cha racteristics.pdf.

In agential realism, the world is not an infinite source of raw material for human exploitation but a strong ethical commitment to response-able scientific practices of care. Response-ability, as articulated by Barad in an interview, is 'a matter of inviting, welcoming, and enabling the response of the Other. That is, what is at issue is response-ability—the ability to respond' (Barad, 2012). This includes responses from the less-human and more-than-human. In terms of tracing the plastic bricks in Fig. 2.1, the point is not to put forward a critique that portrays plastic 'as a common enemy of living things, producing a singular discourse regarding human-plastic relations' (Penfold & Odegard, 2015, p. 51). My interest is in the complex intra-active relationality between human and other-than-human bodies in research and what it means to 'make kin' (Haraway, 2016) with plastic through the stories we tell in early childhood research. As Penfold and Odegard point out, '[k]in making is the process of coming to know plastic in all of its [ethical] complexities and contradictions' and not just cognitively, but through aesthetic enquiry and experimentation (Penfold & Odegard, 2015, p. 60). What is *also* involved in getting to know plastic bricks intimately?

LEGO currently uses about 90,000 tonnes a year of plastics to make its products. The bricks are made from ABS plastic produced from natural gas or crude oil. But the company plans to invest $400 million over the next couple of years to find ways of replacing ABS with 'sustainable' materials by 2030.[48] It already makes the less rigid parts, such as its plants and trees[49] (only up to 2% of its products) from bio-polyethylene derived from Brazilian bioethanol from refined sugarcane.[50]

As iii I am writing this, LEGO already seems to have made a significant breakthrough[51] in producing a sustainable alternative. It has announced that a team of more than 150 materials scientists and engineers[52] have developed 'a prototype LEGO® brick' made from recycled PET plastic bottles.[53] The bricks look the same and supposedly have the same 'quality, safety and play requirements – including clutch power'.

But genuine "sustainability" should include the product's whole "life cycle" and the social and geopolitical conditions under which its raw materials are produced and transported. Even plastics made from plants are not really sustainable. Bioplastics are like plastics produced from any source—recyclable but not biodegradable. They still eventually break up into microplastics. Plastic bricks made with plant-based bio-polyethylene do have a lower carbon footprint than the conventional plastic because sugarcane plants capture carbon dioxide. On the other hand, growing sugar uses large

---

[48] https://www.reuters.com/article/us-lego-sustainability-plastic-idUSKBN2661OO.

[49] See: https://www.theguardian.com/lifeandstyle/2018/mar/02/first-sustainable-lego-pieces-to-go-on-sale.

[50] For why it is important to find alternatives, see how LEGO bricks will be found in the ocean thousands of years from now: https://bigthink.com/surprising-science/bermuda-triangle.

[51] See: https://www.lego.com/fi-fi/aboutus/news/2021/june/prototype-lego-brick-recycled-plastic.

[52] One viable way would be: https://rebrickable.com/.

[53] LEGO Group claims that "On average, a one-litre plastic PET bottle provides enough raw material for ten 2 × 4 LEGO bricks". For the source, see Footnote 51.

quantities of pesticides and fertilisers. Moreover, large sugarcane plantations have highly exploitative and gendered labour conditions (see e.g., Osgood, 2019), and often displace local farmers onto more marginal land.

What will happen to the bricks, even when they have been made from plastic bottles, assuming the continued existence of plastic bottles? Creative solutions have been found, for example, by using old bricks as construction material to playfully fill in the gaps of existing buildings.[54] Plastic's physical properties are ideal for aesthetic experimentation by people of all ages. This also disrupts the science/art binary[55] and provides opportunities for humans to get to know intimately those materials that are part of their everyday lives (Penfold & Odegard, 2015). Getting to know them better might encourage our appreciation for them as something essential to human's healthcare, safety, and standard of living, as well as reducing the demand for wooden products. Assigning such value to them might even discourage us from throwing them away. In summary, tracing the plastic and the material nature of their production, consumption, and management shows that the use of LEGO bricks is always political. They are not "just objects" for human's use in education.

3.8 On /

Barad has generated a profound transdisciplinary philosophical framework that theorises, and simultaneously, enacts a reconfiguration of the relationality between (human) subject and object. Agential realism meets the universe *halfway* in a way that is often misunderstood. It does not offer a 'middle ground' between traditional realism and social constructivism. It rejects the representationalism, individualism, and any kind of foundationalism or theory of transcendence on which both rest (Barad, 2007, p. 408, ftn 1). Like Alice Fulton's poem *Cascade Experiment* referred to in Chap. 2.1 of this book, being in different places in the universe doesn't cause separation, but furthers the entanglement—a 'cutting-together-apart' (Barad, 2007, p. 466).

In agential realism, the world is in/determinate; it is ongoingly worlding itself (Juelskjær et al., 2021, p. 15). "Cuts" made by educators are part of that worlding. Barad calls them *agential cuts*. Not only researching, but learning, teaching, just living[56] is intra-actively engaging in world-making cuts, but not by discrete individual bodies. As Barad contends:

---

[54] With thanks to Jayne Osgood whose feminist new materialist reading of LEGO bricks drew my attention to this particular use of LEGO bricks. In particular because of their hardness and durability they could be used for imaginative use in 'real' constructions. For an example in South Africa, see: https://www.dispatchwork.info/bo-kaap-cape-town/. For the world map: https://www.dispatchwork.info/.

[55] For example, plastic cellophane invites aesthetic experimentation through, e.g., 'colour mixing, transparency, opacity, and texture' (Penfold & Odegard, 2015, p. 57).

[56] There is no intention to set up a binary here between the professional and the private, and between teaching and learning, because these practices are intra-actively entangled (see Chap. 1).

> Cuts are agentially enacted not by willful individuals but by the larger material arrangement of which "we" are a "part." The cuts that we participate in enacting matter. Indeed, ethics cannot be about responding to the other as if the other is the radical outside to the self. Ethics is not a geometrical calculation; "others" are never very far from "us"; "they" and "we" are co-constituted and entangled through the very cuts "we" help to enact. Cuts cut "things" together and apart. Cuts are not enacted from the outside, nor are they ever enacted once and for all. (Barad, 2007, pp. 178–179)

Running through our worldings of the world are 'some sedimented ways of thinking that are so deep that we hardly question them anymore, both in physical theories, but also political theories'.[57] These include engrained habits of thinking about material bodies as simply taking their place as part of environments in the world. Instead, agential realists propose that human and other-than-human bodies are 'intra-actively co-constituted' and 'dynamic reconfigurings' of what exists (Barad, 2007, p. 170). The Lego bricks Zuko is holding are intra-actively co-constituted as 'a camera', thereby symbolically turning the gaze to us researchers. The proposition is to trace the injustices and the violences involved in the agential cuts when the indeterminate is made determinate—even if temporarily. With each cut, particular existences are not permitted or remain invisible. Undoing these injustices is 'not about finding something pure' but involves keeping the questions moving, 'by always asking the prior question'.[58]

Inspired by Jacques Derrida, the agential realist's use of 'justice-to-come' is not about critiquing others for not being just, but acknowledging that every one of us is always already implicated—even in another time or place. Barad acknowledges the influence of their (former) PhD researcher, Astrid Schrader, on their reconfiguring of ontology as *hauntology*. In an ongoing commitment to questions of justice, response-able scientists attend 'to temporality-in-the-making, rather than taking for granted some idea of an externalized notion of time' (Barad, 2007, p. 475, ftn 71). To haunt does not mean to be present, and it is necessary to introduce haunting into the very construction of each concept, including "being" and "time" (Schrader, 2012).

Violence cannot be avoided because all agential cuts pertain to a certain kind of violence, that is, every cut enacts specific exclusions that do not always involve humans. Unlike a Cartesian cut (Barad, 2014), an agential cut is not enacted by intentional human agents but by the material arrangements of which we humans are a part. So, in an ethical, response-able[59] life, we must keep asking how these cuts are made. We need to pay attention to the particular material intra-actions. What kind of violence is produced by *this* differentiating entanglement, rather than *that* one, in their specificities? The forward slash disrupts power-producing binaries. For example, the forward slash in dis/continuity invites us to think of underneath and before, prior to these binaries, and to ask: 'What cuts are being made here that we have such a distinction between continuity and discontinuity?', 'What work does it

---

[57] From Barad's talk *Infinity, Nothingness and the Un/doing of Self* during the Q&A part of the Summerschool 20 July at Cornell University: https://events.cornell.edu/event/karen_barad_inf inity_nothingness_and_the_undoing_of_self.

[58] See Footnote 2.

[59] See Chap. 3.7.

do and what kind of violences does it produce?'.[60] For example, the binary enables material-discursive practices of progress and development.

In the analysis of Fig. 3.1, both the realist and the socio-constructivist studies enact an agential cut between "self" (Zuko) and "other" (the Lego bricks, the researcher, the camera). What kind of violence does developmentalism produce? What are the cuts involved for which we are response-able? Education science and, in the case of the research project that generated Zuko's photo, knowledge production was informed by social constructivism (e.g., nesting scales of data collection: home, family, school), developmental psychology (e.g., measuring children's well-being), and also scientific realism by collecting 'big data' through quantitative surveys and holding on to representational notions of objectivity. Material-discursive readings of the phenomenon pay attention to the fine details of the entanglement without setting up a binary between representation and nonrepresentation, articulated through a forward slash in non/representation. Nonrepresentational readings only exist in relation to representational readings. They are the very condition of each other. In the next chapter, the difference it makes to choose one over the other is explored in the context of teaching and assessing a master's course in higher education in Finland (Chap. 4.4).

Moving away from a socio-cultural symbolic 'correct' reading of the image to a transdisciplinary tracing of relationalities within the phenomenon produces different subjectivities and "definitions" of concepts that always already includes the material. Moreover, so-called 'symbolic' readings, are, in fact, "matterphorical" readings of texts (Barad & Gandorfer, 2021). Matter and meaning cannot be separated because meaning-making is always already a specific material doing or enactment of the world in its iterative becoming. It is for this reason that different readings, e.g., a socio-cultural and an agential realist, are not mutually exclusive. Other modes of analysis are always already threaded through one another, but they can be articulated differently through particular agential cuts for which the researcher is response-able. Importantly, objectivity is worked towards, not by disentangling and disengaging the subject from the object (as in much research), but by taking responsibility for how the knowing subject and her apparatuses (e.g., digital technology) are always already ontologically entangled in what is produced.

Questions of space, time, and matter are intimately connected, indeed entangled, with questions of justice. Photography as apparatus already participates in producing data. This is radically different from a scientific realist paradigm whereby the photo of Zuko counts as evidence of the child's existence and agency in the world, separate from the agencies of observation. Zuko as a research subject is thus seen as an individually existing body bounded by the surface of his skin that separates him from other human and other-than-human bodies. However, these models already assume that what is represented (a child holding Lego bricks) exists independently of all practices of representing (Barad, 2007, p. 46), including the binaries that are already given (e.g., child/adult, culture/nature, inner/outer). This chapter puts at stake the model itself—the mirror between culture and nature.

---

[60] See Footnote 2.

The diffractive analysis of the photo in Fig. 3.1 shows that an agential realist does not embrace epistemic, cultural, or moral relativism (Sect. 3.1). It is certainly not the case that 'anything goes'. The 'world kicks back' (Chap. 1.1), not in the sense of individualised agency, but agency as 'distributed over nonhuman as well as human forms' (Barad, 2007, pp. 214–215). Not everything is possible at every given moment. Interior and exterior, past, present, and future are iteratively enfolded and reworked, but never eliminated (and never fixed). Intra-actions reconfigure the possibilities for change. In fact, intra-actions not only reconfigure spacetimematter but reconfigure what is possible. Barad (2007, p. 182) powerfully argues that ethicality is part of the fabric of the world; the call to respond and be responsible is part of what is. What flashes up in this chapter is why it matters in education research.

Many, many more questions cascade. But the chapter has run out of space. In Chapter four we switch to teaching and ponder over the implications for reworking the key concepts in this chapter for teaching in all phases of education, con/texts, and assessment.

The diffractive reading of Figs. 2.1 and 3.1 through one another has been very generative and barely started. The historicity of the Lego brick caught the attention, the land (Pinelands) has had a (short) response, the concept of child has been engaged with, but in/finite stories still need to be told, including the historicity of Zuko and the iPhone that took the photo. To be dis/continued.

References

Barad, K. (1996). Meeting the universe halfway: Realism and social constructivism without contradiction. In L. H. Nelson & J. Nelson (Eds.), *Feminism, science, and the philosophy of science* (pp. 161–94). Kluwer Press.

Barad, K. (2003). Posthumanist performativity: Toward an understanding of how matter comes to matter. *Signs: Journal of Women in Culture and Society, 28*(31), 801–831.

Barad, K. (2007). *Meeting the universe halfway: Quantum physics and the entanglement of matter and meaning.* Duke University Press.

Barad, K. (2010). Quantum entanglements and hauntological relations of inheritance: Dis/continuities, spacetime enfoldings, and justice-to-come. *Derrida Today, 3*(2), 240–68. https://doi.org/10.3366/drt.2010.0206

Barad, K. (2011). Erasers and erasures: Pinch's unfortunate 'uncertainty principle.' *Social Studies of Science, 41*(3), 443–454.

Barad, K. (2012). Intra-actions: An interview with Karen Barad by Adam Kleinman. *Mousse* #34 June, 76–81.

Barad, K. (2014). Diffracting diffractions: Cutting together-apart. *Parallax, 20*(3), 168–187.

Barad, K. (2015). TransMaterialities: Trans*/matter/realities and queer political imaginings. *GLQ, 21*(2–3), 387–422.

Barad, K. (2017). What flashes up: Theological-political-scientific fragments. In C. Keller & M.-J. Rubenstein (Eds.), *Entangled worlds: Religion, science, and new materialisms* (pp. 21–88). Fordham University Press.

Barad, K. (2018). Troubling time/s and ecologies of nothingness: On the im/possibilities of living and dying in the void. In M. Fritsch, P. Lynes, & D. Wood (Eds.), *Ecodeconstruction: Derrida and environmental philosophy* (pp. 206–248). Fordham University Press.

Barad, K. (2019). After the end of the world: Entangled nuclear colonialisms, matters of force, and the material force of justice. *Theory & Event, 22*(3), 524–550.

Barad, K., & Gandorfer, D. (2021). Political desirings: Yearnings for mattering (,) differently. *Theory & Event, 24*(1), 14–66.

Carle, E. (1969). *The very hungry caterpillar.* Putnam.

Colebrook, C. (2020). Fast violence, revolutionary violence: Black Lives Matter and the 2020 Pandemic. *Journal of Bioethical Inquiry.* https://doi.org/10.1007/s11673-020-10024-9

Deleuze, G., & Guattari, F. (2014). *A thousand plateaus.* Translated and a foreword by B. Massumi. Bloomsbury.

Haraway, D. (2008). *When species meet.* University of Minnesota Press.

Haraway, D. (2016). *Staying with the trouble: Making kin in the Chthulucene.* Duke University Press.

Haraway, D. (1988). Situated knowledges: The science question in feminism and the privilege of partial perspective. *Feminist Studies, 14*, 575–599.

Haynes, J., & Murris, K. (2019). Taking age out of play: Children's animistic philosophising through a picturebook. *The Oxford Literary Review, 41*(2), 290–309. https://doi.org/10.3366/olr.2019.0284

Hollin, G., Giraud, E., Forsyth, I., & Potts, T. (2017). (Dis)entangling barad: Materialisms and ethics. *Social Studies of Science, 47*(6), 918–941.

Hultman, K., & Lenz Taguchi, H. (2010). Challenging anthropocentric analysis of visual data: A relational materialist methodological approach to educational research. *International Journal of Qualitative Studies in Education, 23*(5), 525–542.

Juelskjær, M., Plauborg, H., & Adrian, S. (2021). *Dialogues on agential realism: Engaging in worldings through research practice.* Routledge.

Juelskjær, M., & Schwennesen, N. (2012). *Intra-active entanglements: An interview with Karen Barad. Kvinder, Koen og Forskning, 21*(1–2), 10–23.

MacLure, M. (2013). Researching without representation? Language and materiality in post-qualitative methodology. *Special Issue: Post-Qualitative Research International Journal of Qualitative Studies in Education, 26*(6), 658–667.

Marsh, J., Murris, K., Ng'ambi, D., Parry, R., Scott, F., Thomsen, B. S., Bishop, J., Bannister, C., Dixon, K., Giorza, T., Peers, J., Titus, S., Da Silva, H., Doyle, G., Driscoll, A., Hall, L., Hetherington, A., Krönke, M., Margary, T., … Woodgate, A. (2020). Children, technology and play. *Billund*, Denmark: The LEGO Foundation. ISBN: 978-87-999589-7-9. https://www.legofoundation.com/media/2855/children-tech-and-play_full-report.pdf

Murris, K. (2016). The posthuman child: Educational transformation through philosophy with picturebooks. In G. Dahlberg and P. Moss (Eds.), *Contesting early childhood series.* Routledge.

Murris, K. (2021). The 'Missing Peoples' of critical posthumanism and new materialism. In K. Murris (Ed.), *Navigating the postqualitative, new materialist and critical posthumanist terrain across disciplines: An introductory guide* (pp. 62–85). Routledge.

Murris, K., & Crowther, J. (2018). 'Digging and diving for treasure: Erasures, silences and secrets'. In K. Murris & J. Haynes (Eds.), *Literacies, literature and learning: Reading classrooms differently* (pp. 149–173). Routledge Research Monographs Series.

Murris, K., & Menning, S. F. (2019). Videography and decolonizing education. *Video Journal of Education and Pedagogy, 4*, 1–8. On-line, open access journal. Accessible on: https://brill.com/view/journals/vjep/4/1/vjep.4.issue-1.xml

Murris, K., & Reynolds, B. (2018). A manifesto posthuman child: De/colonising childhood through reconfiguring the human [Video]. Youtube. https://www.youtube.com/watch?v=ikN-LGhBawQ

Murris, K., Reynolds, R.-A., da Silva, H., & de Souza, L. A. (2021). Untidying child development with a picturebook: Disrupting colonizing binary logic in teacher education. In N. J. Yelland, L. Peters, M. Tesar, & M. S. Perez (Eds.), *The SAGE handbook of global childhoods* (pp. 397–410). Sage.

Nelson, L. H., & Nelson, J. (Eds.). (1997). *Feminism, Science and the Philosophy of Science.* Kluwer.

Osgood, J. (2019). Materialised reconfigurations of gender in early childhood: Playing Seriously with Lego. In J. Osgood & K. Robinson (Eds.), *Feminists researching gendered childhoods, feminist thought in childhood research series* (pp. 85–108). Bloomsbury.
Penfold, L. K., & Odegard, N. (2015). Making kin with plastic through aesthetic experimentation. *Journal of Childhood Studies, 46*(2), 51–65.
Pinch, T. (2011). Karen Barad, quantum mechanics, and the paradox of mutual exclusivity. *Social Studies of Science, 41*(3), 431–441.
Rouse, J. (2004). Barad's feminist naturalism. *Hypatia, 19*(1), 142–161.
Schrader, A. (2012). Haunted measurements: Demonic work and time in experimentation. *Differences: A Journal of Feminist Cultural Studies, 23*(3), 119–160.
Sellberg, K., & Hinton, P. (2016). Introduction: The possibilities of feminist quantum thinking. *Rhizomes: Cultural Studies in Emerging Knowledge*, 30. https://doi.org/10.20415/rhiz/030.i01
St. Pierre, E. A. (2011). Post qualitative research: The critique and the coming after. In N. K. Denzin & Y. S. Lincoln (Eds.), *The SAGE handbook of qualitative research* (4th ed., pp. 611–625). Sage Publications.

Chapter 4
Diffraction as Childlike Methodology in Education

4.1 Introduction—Topology Matters

Chapter 3 presents the idea that non/representational[1] methodologies take account of the fact that we are ontologically part of that nature we seek to understand. The diffractive methodology is enacted through the agential realist analysis of a photograph of "six-year-old" Zuko (Fig. 3.1). The image is read as a Baradian phenomenon—not as an object in spacetime as "container" of things, but diffractively through Fig. 2.1. The latter articulates Karen Barad "as" constellation, not an individualised, bounded body *in* space and time (Chap. 3). The topology of spacetime containers is the meta/physics of Western philosophy at least as old as Democritus' atom theory (Chap. 3.1). As argued elsewhere (Murris, 2017, p. 132):

> the containment model for bodily boundaries and selves might be more typical of male experience, which has shaped the western metaphysical notion of self and self-identity: bodies as containers and selves as autonomous (Battersby, 1998, p.54) – a body that is One and not the Other. In metaphysical constructions of self, philosophers have bypassed the female body which "is messy, fleshy and gapes open to otherness – with otherness 'within', as well as 'without'". (Battersby, 1998, p. 59)

Karen Barad's diffractive reading of quantum physics, especially Quantum Field Theory (QFT), troubles the topology implicit in dominant container metaphors. Articulated powerfully through one of the key concepts, *agential separability*, agential realism rejects the geometries of absolute outsides and insides. The concept 'opens up a much larger space that is more appropriately thought of as a dynamic and ever-changing topology' (Barad, 2007, pp. 76–77). Agential separability reworks matter

---

[1] The forward slash in "non/representational", like all "/" in this book, articulates an ontological commitment to "cutting together-apart", rather than a Cartesian cut (see especially Chap. 3.8). It expresses a posthumanist commitment to diffracting through all (adult) western binaries without claiming this can ever be achieved. It is ongoing, iterative work for justice-to-come (see e.g., Sect. 4.1.1).

© The Author(s), under exclusive license to Springer Nature Singapore Pte Ltd. 2022
K. Murris, *Karen Barad as Educator*,
SpringerBriefs on Key Thinkers in Education,
https://doi.org/10.1007/978-981-19-0144-7_4

as *exteriority within phenomena* (Barad, 2007, p. 236). In a footnote, Barad argues why topology *matters* as follows:

> Although spatiality is often thought of geometrically, particularly in terms of the characteristics of enclosures (like size and shape), this is only one way of thinking about space. Topological features of manifolds can be extremely important. For example, **two points that seem far apart when viewed geometrically may, given a particular connectivity of the manifold**, be understood as being proximate to each other (as, for example, in the case of cosmological objects called "wormholes") when topological considerations are taken into account. (Barad, 2007, p. 436, ftn 78)

The critical issue here is that these 'two points' (and the *fact* that they are in relation) might not be visible, sensed, known, or even articulatable by a human. For example, women living together for some time start to synchronise their periods without even being aware of it. Their bodies are in relation and connected in more ways than those accessible to humans (e.g., the moon's influence on the menstrual cycle). Yet, in the education literature, there is scant attention paid to the body's materiality. This includes the school as a body, how it affects learning and well-being, and why this matters. As an example, the menstruating body, and more generally the body that "leaks", is not regarded as a 'normal body' (McGregor, 2020, p. 383) and rarely features in the literature. This is especially true of teachers' leaky bodies. Scholarly publications and policy reports discuss the subject of school toilets only concerning children, and only then from medical, hygiene, and developmental perspectives that might improve their school attendance and cognitive gains (UNICEF and World Health Organization, 2018; WaterAid, 2018).

The entangled relation between space, time, and matter connects with matters of justice (in the case of toilets in South Africa, see e.g., Rivers, 2017). Topology concerns itself with connectivity and boundaries. It provokes geopolitical readings of space, including the land when reading for example, the image of Zuko playing with plastic bricks in Chapter three (Fig. 3.1)—even when there is no land visible in the photograph. Diffraction troubles the human-centred notion of vision.

The fundamental dis/continuity (Chap. 3.8) of Quantum Field Theory (QFT) troubles the nature of difference: '"Otherness" is an entangled relation of difference'[2] (Barad, 2007, p. 236). As a *spacetimematter* manifold, there are no linear causal relations between one thing and another (Chap. 3.3)—only 'ongoing topological dynamics of enfolding': 'phenomena are forever being reenfolded and reformed' (Barad, 2007, p. 177). This also holds for relations "between" teacher and learner and the pedagogical interventions (*agential cuts*[3]) that are, in fact, "intra-ventions": teacher, learner, atmosphere, international assessment, clock time, policies, parents, land etc. These *relata* (Barad, 2007, pp. 137–138) are not autonomously existing

---

[2] Like Donna Haraway and others, Barad diffracts through Trin Minh-ha's concept of 'inappropriate/d Others' (Barad, 2014, p. 172), troubling notions of "First" and "Other", including the idea that they (Barad) would be the First agential realist.

[3] See more about agential cuts in Chap. 3.8.

entities that preexist their relations. They are dynamically and iteratively enfolded into one another. The body of a teacher is ("like" that of)[4] a *pregnant stingray.*

"Like" the brittlestar in Chap. 3, the stingray is another animal that teaches us to rework bodily boundaries, and comes to the rescue in reconfiguring education. Elsewhere, iii diffract the performative practices of the self-stinging stingray, the midwife, and the pregnant human body through one another (Murris, 2017). Troubling the existence of independent bounded bodies, Barad (2011) points out that the neuronal receptor cells in stingrays make it possible for these creatures to anticipate a message which has not yet arrived—a kind of clairvoyance. The concept of clairvoyance troubles unilinear time as it strikes like a lightning flash and crystallises (Barad, 2017) into the figuration of "the" diffractive educator. Educating is a performative world-making practice that disrupts unilinear time: *past, present, and future bleed through one another in the thick-now of any moment* (Chap. 2.4). Confounding the logic of causality, stingrays unlock themselves before this is (apparently) necessary (Barad, 2011).

iii explore elsewhere the figuration of the diffractive educator through a photo my camera took of a heron. Standing in the river Rhine, the heron creates a diffraction pattern in the water (Fig. 1 in Murris, 2018, p. 3). Notably, the way these animals, the brittlestar (Chap. 3.1.1), stingray, and heron are "used" as "characters" in "my" writing is not as metaphors or analogies but as *homologies.* The former assumes representationalism and the culture/nature binary (see Chap. 3.1). Analogical thinking involves comparing and contrasting two ontologically separate entities: animals and humans. With human intelligence as the norm with which to measure any intelligence, it is "obvious" that, for example, herons can't be teachers. This is because they have little intelligence (a "bird brain") and none of the self-reflective consciousness required for being a (reflexive) teacher. This sounds like "commonsense"? But the problem with metaphorical thinking is that it is representational. So, in this case, the teacher (read: culture) and the heron (read: nature) are assumed to be at an ontological distance from one another (see Chap. 3.1). The human who thinks this connection between teacher and heron *re-presents* the heron *as* the teacher through language or other symbolic sign systems does so *without attributing teacher qualities to the heron.* In contrast, animals (and later, "child") are not metaphorical resources for adult humans to use here, but articulate how the world worlds itself, or put differently, how the world is iteratively becoming.

It might be "counter-intuitive", as is typical of agential realism, but the diffractive teacher is part of that nature we seek to understand (Chap. 3). As *a matter of fact* (and value), the teacher and heron are basically *doing the same thing.* They create diffraction patterns as performative world-making practices. Barad states that agential realism is a realism that is not defined by the 'representation of an independent reality but about the real consequences, interventions, creative possibilities, and responsibilities of intra-acting within and as part of the world'.[5] Now, if this is indeed

---

[4] Putting this subclause in brackets articulates the idea that this is not a case of analogical thinking—see below.

[5] This description of agential realism is from Instagram #karenbarad (15.11.2021).

how the world *is* in its iterative becoming, including our own actions as pedagogues, what are the implications for teaching and learning? As current curricula are steeped in practices of reflection and reflexivity, how does diffraction reconfigure curriculum development in all phases of education? How do posthumanist educators move away from the notion of the teacher as the "expert"[6]? How does it work in education when knowledge production is understood as performative and an iterative world-making practice? How can we re-imagine the role of the educator?

Let's continue with enquiring into these questions by re-turning first to a very educative interview with Barad. In response to a question posed by Daniela Gandorfer, Barad reminds us that, some might say, "even" in quantum physics, claims to knowledge remain open for further enquiry. This is not only by humans, because theory (and the other-than-human more broadly) itself responds to the world in its iterative reconfiguring, and is always dynamic and on the move (literally):

> One crucial point not to be missed is that there is no "the quantum theory" (just as there is no "the political theory"). While the latter is taken for granted; some people insist on pointing to "what quantum theory **says**." (Barad in Barad & Gandorfer, 2021, p. 23; my emphasis)

It is crucial to keep asking the prior questions, and Barad proposes in the context of QFT:

> to shift the approach, to not frame the work as "the analysis of ...", that is, to assume a Newtonian analytic (where analysis-at-a-distance already cuts the analysis short). I suggested using quantum physics to unearth what underlies this, and to do so in a way that respects the understanding of physics and politics as always already inside one another. In particular, in **tracing the entanglements of this strange topology (where each is inside the other)** it was necessary to open up the notion of "the physics", as well as the political, to being reworked. (Barad & Gandorfer, 2021, pp. 22–23; my emphases)

The "knots" that follow in this chapter continue to respond to the important questions raised above by exploring the diffractive methodology as practised. Chapter 3 traces some entanglements with/in a photo "of" Zuko, moving the transdisciplinary analysis from reading the photograph as an object, to "meeting" the image as a phenomenon, a constellation—meeting "the universe halfway". In this chapter, nonlinear knots[7] diffract through diffractive educational practices. They include an "empty" (k)not at the "end" of this book, an articulation of a 'strange topology' where past, present, and future are inside one another, silently rupturing ageist, ableist, racist, extractive, and settler-colonial logics in education.

We have seen in Chap. 3 how working with topological manifolds through figurations such as constellations crystallises a very different way of doing education research. This chapter focuses on the diffractive methodology "itself". Of course, agential realism "itself" implies that "its" methodologies are not statically One and the Same, but dynamically enfold as part of material-discursive worlding processes we as educators are part of (as well as "our" theories and practices). Leaving the more detailed writing about diffraction

---

[6] See for the concept of the "expert" Chap. 1, and for representationalism Chap. 3.

[7] See Chap. 1 for an explanation of how the knotty structure works in this book.

to the "last" chapter is deliberate. It disrupts styles of writing and teaching that proceed unilinearly with a hierarchical structure because it positions the author as the expert: *explaining*-theories-by-*giving*-definitions-of-concepts-and-then-*applying*-them-to-empirical-data-or-by-*giving*-examples. Most academic writing, assessment practices, and other aspects of our educational system are dominated by this representationalist structure (in)formed by deep dualism (see Murris, 2016, Ch. 1).

In contrast, the structure of *Karen Barad as Educator* articulates a nonlinear, dis/continuous pedagogy by deliberately not starting with definitions of concepts, but lets them breathe as a response-able practice: 'It is what the diffractive methodology tries to do, namely working with concepts and at the same time opening them up, aerating them, so they can continue to breathe' (Barad in Barad & Gandorfer, 2021, p. 31).

Inspired by Karen Barad "as" educator,[8] teaching diffractively avoids moving from the simple and complex with the teacher as an expert who inducts the learner into new ideas and who provides an imaginary for a different kind of criticality. In conversation,[9] Karen Barad comments that there are many different kinds of learning, but the problem with the transmission model is that discussions often focus on what is wrong with the transmitter, or the receiver, or the signal, rather than with the model itself.

Guided by recent interviews with Karen Barad (Barad & Gandorfer, 2021; Juel-skjær et al., 2021) and educational events,[10] this chapter mobilises the diffractive methodology to diffract early childhood education and the concept of "child" through the methodology.[11] Diffracting through Derrida brings about the interference pattern that diffraction "itself" is a *childlike methodology* and *pedagogy*. Although Barad in *Meeting the Universe Halfway* (2007) does not explicitly refer to pedagogy, it is not difficult to see how agential realism would theorise pedagogical encounters as dynamic differentiating childlike intra-actions. Through the *doing* of the theory and enactment of diffraction *at the same time,* this chapter "itself" diffracts theory

---

[8] See Chap. 1 for troubling the reading of the phrase "Karen Barad as educator" as signifying the person Karen Barad as an individual identity *in* space and time.

[9] This is how iii re-call Karen Barad's response when Theresa Giorza had asked them to comment on learning as a worlding practice, rather than transmission. For the occasion see Footnote 17 in Chap. 1.

[10] This chapter in particular benefits from Malou Juelskaer's visit to the University of Oulu in September 2021. Funded by the university, Malou taught a hybrid course for doctorate students on Agential Realism and Decolonising Education. The course included a guest lecture by Astrid Schrader. The course was recorded and my dynamic and iteratively developing understandings of the diffractive methodology benefited profoundly from re-turning to "this event" that is still open (also, thanks to technology).

[11] To do justice to the complexity, the diffraction pattern is as follows: Barad's take on the diffractive methodology is a diffraction of diffraction (Barad, 2014) and my diffractive reading of education through the methodology diffracts through that paper. In addition, it diffracts through Schrader's writing and presentation on hauntology (see previous footnote).

and practice, early childhood education and higher education, teacher and learner, adult and child. In doing so, it puts forward a passionate plea to de/colonise higher education by adopting the diffractive methodology in teaching, learning, assessment, and education research. Such a higher education is a *childlike education*.[12]

4.1.1 *"The" Diffractive Methodology*

As we have seen in Chap. 2, the diffractive methodology has been developed (is developing and continuing to develop) intra-actively with other feminist thinkers (e.g., at the university in Santa Cruz), particularly by diffracting through physicist Niels Bohr's influential complementarity theory. His famous two-slit diffraction experiment (Barad, 2007, pp. 81–84) made evident that under certain conditions, light behaves like a particle (as Newton thought), and under other conditions, behaves like a wave. In other words, electrons are neither particles nor waves; wave and particle are *not inherent attributes of objects*, but are the 'nature of the observed phenomenon changes with corresponding changes in the apparatus' that measures it (Barad, 2007, p. 106). Electrons and the differences "between" them are neither "here" nor "there", "this" or "that", "one" or the "other" or any other binary type of difference. And Barad (2014, pp. 174–175) claims that what holds for an electron also holds for a human animal: '…as far as we know the world is not broken up into distinct regions each with different physical laws and realities' (Barad, 2007, p. 471, ftn 47). In other words, the concepts "macro" and "micro" 'already presume a given spatial scale' (Barad, 2010, p. 240).[13] Diffraction as methodology articulates an intra-active relational ontology.[14]

As Malou Juelskjær and colleagues put it strikingly: 'diffraction, when enacted in agential realism, is primarily a quantum-physical phenomenon related to how the world worlds itself' (Juelskjær et al., 2021, p. 12). As a quantum entanglement, 'each moment is an infinite multiplicity' (Barad, 2014, p. 169). The Baradian notion of quantum entanglement troubles all binaries at their very core (Chap. 2.2), including— the distinction "between" adult and child—particularly important for this chapter (and education).

It is highly relevant for education that the non/representational methodology of diffraction de(con)structs (Chap. 3.6) how we tend to read texts. It troubles the ontology of texts as independently existing bodies with precise "edges" and "boundaries" separated from their "context" and "other" texts. Texts are always already in relation, which changes how we think about "critique". A diffractive reading is different from (a certain kind of) critique in that text/oeuvres/approaches/viewpoints are relationally read *through* each other, looking for and strengthening creative and

---

[12] My ideas about a childlike education are very much inspired by the Philosophy with Children movement and in particular the scholarship of Joanna Haynes, David Kennedy and Walter Kohan.

[13] For an important discussion on matters of scale, see Chap. 3.3 and ftn 42.

[14] See Chap. 1.3 about Intra-active relational ontology.

unexpected provocations. Reconfiguring critique is particularly important in higher education. In a paper with Vivienne Bozalek, for example, we engage with diffraction as a relational, feminist form of academic engagement (Murris & Bozalek, 2019a). Our response to Serge Hein's unsubstantiated critique on Barad presents us with the opportunity to diffractively explore how the relational ontologies of Barad and Gilles Deleuze speak to one another as an alternative academic practice of reading texts. We also refer to other examples of such response-able readings that do more justice to texts' entangled relationalities. We then formulate a series of Whiteheadian "propositions" for adopting the diffractive methodology in education and life in general (Murris & Bozalek, 2019b).

Derrida's notion of 'justice-to-come' that both Karen Barad and Astrid Schrader diffract through is useful here. Justice-to-come implies that "we" as academics, authors, teachers, thinkers, supervisors, students, and other human and other-than-human earthlings are always already implicated—even in another time or place (Schrader in Juelskjær et al., 2021). Barad modestly admits to not being the 'First agential realist'.[15] As an open, dynamic philosophy, the influence of Astrid Schrader on the diffractive methodology has been significant, especially for the notion of justice-to-come and de/colonising education. In other words, how Barad proposes concepts are developed collaboratively (and not just as an activity reserved for humans) also holds for the concept of diffraction.

In an interview, Astrid Schrader, a former student of both Haraway and Barad, describes her initial interest in agential realism as an opportunity for combining notions of responsibility and objectivity in science. And then, she says, 'luckily Karen Barad just happened to show up at the right time in Santa Cruz, when I was about to begin my second year as a graduate student in the History of Consciousness' (Schrader in Juelskjær et al., 2021, p. 48). Schrader explains what she likes about Haraway's notion of diffraction in 1997 and how she diffracts through it in her own doctorate research:

> "diffraction patterns record the history of interaction, interference, reinforcement, difference. Diffraction is about heterogeneous history, not about originals. Unlike reflections, diffractions do not displace the same elsewhere".

> While this sounds very similar, there is a crucial difference between these two notions of diffraction: Barad's introduction of entanglement matters. Barad expresses this with the help of a distinction between geometrical optics and quantum optics, or classical and physical optics. Many of the insights of agential realism follow from treating **diffraction as a quantum phenomenon**. One could say that, while Haraway's notion of diffraction did not consider the quantum world, it was rather more attuned to the historical. So, there was something in Haraway's notion of diffraction that I didn't want to let go of, and that was her reference to **the recording of the history of interference patterns** that wasn't highlighted in Barad's quantum physical treatment. So, there was something I wanted to do with that recording of history, **the temporal aspect of Haraway's notion of diffraction**. (Schrader in Juelskjær et al., 2021, p. 51; my emphases)

---

[15] See Footnote 2.

Schrader's diffracting through Haraway's and Barad's[16] articulations of diffraction materialises the *hauntological version of diffraction*. Schrader explains why it matters:

> Derrida's notion of inheritance then became more helpful for me, what he describes as a task that remains before us (Derrida, 1994, p. 54). This was then the background to my re-reading of Barad's description of the quantum erasure effect in hauntological terms, literally (or physically) combining diffraction and deconstruction in "Haunted measurements". (see Schrader, 2012)

This diffractive collaborative work on diffraction as a concept illustrates how diffraction works as a feminist methodology and how it iteratively reconfigures and reworks not only critique but also justice as continuously strived for and never finally achieved (Juelskjær et al., 2021, p. 134). In an interview (Barad & Gandorfer, 2021, p. 38), Barad elaborates that they (Barad) don't reject critique out of hand because it is 'an important political tool'. This is the case, for example, in Bohr's critique of Heisenberg's uncertainty principle. We just need to 'push back on certain conceptions of critique' (Barad in Barad & Gandorfer, 2021, p. 38): 'it must be an immanent critique, that is, not from without, but from within and as part of these very practices' (Juelskjær et al., 2021, p. 124).

Diffractive criticality is responsive and response-able; it allows the "other" (human *and* nonhuman) to respond (Chap. 3.7). Whereas reflection focuses upon sameness and separateness, diffraction is about 'reading insights through one another in attending to and responding to the details and specificities of relations of difference and how they matter', while also focusing on the multiplicity of temporalities in any given "moment" (Barad, 2007, p. 71). The notion of "thick-time" appears in Barad's later writings, also inspired by Judith Butler and Walter Benjamin (Barad, 2017). And Derrida's (Schrader's) hauntology is threaded through the notion of *temporal diffraction*—an essential one for de/colonising education as we will explore in this chapter, using examples from my own teaching in higher education.

In Chap. 3, Barad's work inspires a different doing of education research through the diffractive reading of a photo of Zuko (Fig 3.1) diffracted through Fig 2.1 as a "constellation". The explosive diffractive methodology blasts away the dominant developmental orientation to research involving young children. Agential realism not only affects our research practices, but it also educates our pedagogies and assessment practices in all phases of education. As if that weren't enough, agential realism troubles *the very distinctions* that structure these educational settings: higher/early, formal/informal, expert/novice, teacher/student, and adult/child. The concept of age works to keep these power-producing binaries in place, and disrupting them is part of an education that is response-able. How can we engage our students

---

[16] Barad (in Juelskjær et al., 2021, p. 120) explains that diffraction connects the relational ontology of agential realism with a methodology: 'a key methodological question for my work was: what methodology might there be for putting different insights into conversation with one another that does not belie a relational ontology?' They then 'found the answer in a talk by Donna Haraway in 1994 about her interest in diffraction published later in her book, *Modest_Witness*'. Yet for Barad, Haraway uses diffraction as a *semiotic* category (see Barad, 2007, p. 416, ftn 2).

of any age in educational opportunities that allow them to 'walk around in concepts' (Barad & Gandorfer, 2021, p. 31) and to engage in childlike de(con)struction? The remainder of this chapter gives an example from teaching master's students in Education at a Finnish university who explore how the childlike diffractive methodology de/colonises education.

4.2 On De/colonisation

Discourses about decolonisation are about examining the various ways in which coloniality manifests itself in producing and communicating knowledge and meaning-making (Bhattacharya, 2009; Patel, 2016; Smith, 1999). Its focus is on the important topics of racism, sexism, classism, and ableism, and increasingly on land (e.g., Nxumalo, 2020; Sundberg, 2014; Tuck et al., 2014; Watts, 2013). The usual referent of "human" is that of the adult human, not the younger human. Decolonisation tends not to include a specific focus on children and age (Murris, 2016, 2021). The fundamental functions and needs of child bodies are often overlooked—even in agential realism.

Moreover, the idea that the 'West' in Western science or philosophy refers to a homogenous unit is at odds with agential realism and requires reworking. Indeed, it could be argued that (ironically) Karen Barad is (and is not) a Western philosopher in the same way Derrida was, and Nietzsche and Heidegger. Barad's diffractive reading of Western academic philosophy is from "within" and not from "without". Arguably, it is Anglo-American philosophy and not Continental philosophy that takes the atomistic individualised human subject as its ontological starting point. Still, even that is a simplification; see, for example, American Pragmatism and Peircean semiotics (Semetsky, 2015). It may be more helpful to refer to a *metaphysics of individualism* as "the problem" rather than Western meta/physics when critiquing humanist education (Snaza, 2015). After all, the idea that we cannot detach ourselves from a world that we are part of ontologically is not new in Western philosophy,[17] despite the fact that Donna Haraway (1988, p. 581) is often quoted as the originator of the idea that we cannot observe the world from a neutral perspective.

The way in which Haraway puts the complexity and danger of generalising groups of individuals is particularly appealing (Haraway, 2016, p. 175, ftn 12):

> Outside (and inside) the odd thing named the West, there are myriad histories, philosophies and practices – some civilizational, some urban, some neither – that propose living and dying in other knots and patterns that do not presume isolated, much less binary, unities and polarities that then need to be brought into connection. Variously and dangerously configured relationality is just what is.

Barad and Haraway's solution to Western ills is far from straightforward: "convergences", diffraction, and a reconfiguring of relationality, rather than focusing on

---

[17] See e.g. Martin Heidegger's critique of Western philosophy's preoccupation with things (*Seiendes*), rather than being (*Sein*) in *Being and Time* (1979).

identities. For example, Haraway's suggestion to diffractively read Western ecological sciences through Buddhism is intriguing (Haraway, 2016, pp. 175–176, ftn12). Diffraction thinks of difference outside a metaphysics of individualism and diffracts through Daoist yin/yang thinking (no comparison or analogy) (Zhao, 2019).

Barad suggests that through diffraction, you gain 'insights into how particular ways of framing things contribute to the very constitution of "this" and "that" as always already in relation to one another' (Juelskjær et al., 2021, p. 120). Although Barad refers to the contrasting pair 'this' and 'that' and not explicitly to the "West" and "East" binary, methodologically, you can make any contrasting concepts converse with one other. This *ontological* relationality is expressed through the forward slash "/" (Chap. 3.8), also in de/colonisation, which is tied to the concept of "justice-to-come". Colonisation and decolonisation are intricately entwined: one cannot exist without the other.

It is im/possible to say where West starts and East ends, and vice versa. They are more than locations on a map or about dis/identification of particular groups or people. Each concept is profoundly political and tied to specific, traceable material-discursive practices. It is better to regard West and East as phenomena rather than as bounded entities (West versus East); otherwise, the fabric of relationality itself is at stake. Agential realism allows us to see theories, practices, everything as always in relation and not to generalise about groups of people, including "children". It is also im/possible to say where "child" ends, and "adult" starts or vice versa—even when referring to childhood as a phase in a human's life (Murris & Kohan, 2020).

Barad's more recent writings are of particular interest for educators interested in de/colonisation. As already mentioned, Derrida's (Schrader's) hauntology, threaded through the diffractive methodology, brings to the fore that diffraction is not only about multiple spaces, but also involves multiple temporalities. This includes Barad's claim that there is no void that is determinately empty. In an interview, Barad draws one of the important political implications of Quantum Field Theory (QFT) for de/colonisation—troubling the idea and practice of 'figuring the void as empty and devoid of all mattering' (Barad & Gandorfer, 2021, p. 31). Not letting the void speak is a form of 'colonial violence':

> the irrepressible question/ing of the void is far from immaterial' and 'it speaks (and does not speak!)—it yearns to express the in/expressible—(to) the very im/possibility for non/existence. (Barad & Gandorfer, 2021, p. 31)

Barad (2012, p. 5) suggests a particular kind of listening with/in the void with apparatuses tuned in to 'every subtle detail'. This kind of transindividual "fleshy, leaking and opening-up to others" dis/embodied listening by the (pregnant) body (Sect. 4.1.1) involves not only listening to what humans as a matter of fact express (e.g., through words, gestures) but being attuned to what is not "there", yet still has the potential to be articulated (the virtual). This "intuitive" pedagogical work could, for example, include silence (of human voices), transmodal opportunities for the articulation of ideas, small group work, dance, singing, or going for a walk. How the virtual actualises itself cannot be predicted or planned for. The de/constructive move "away" from language is a fundamental feature of the diffractive methodology.

For Derrida, language needs to be undone from *adult* constructions as a philosophical kind of *unlearning*. In that sense, 'deconstruction is childlike' but also 'the genius of childhood' (Derrida in Cixous & Derrida, 2019, p. 153). In a recent interview, he derides how his methodology of deconstruction sometimes passes as a 'kind of linguisticist mania'. And indeed, there is rich diffractive potential in his notion of *childlike and animallike deconstruction*. Derrida explains that:

> deconstruction began by *suspecting the authority of language*, of verbal language, and even the trace, which is not yet, which is not language, which is not verbality, which is not human, so, the child, *infans*, is not man. *Infans* is what is not yet man. Hence the question of the animal which is everywhere, no? Between the child and the animal, there are obviously all the links you imagine. Deconstruction is animal from this point of view. It is childlike and animal-like. (Derrida in Cixous & Derrida, 2019, p. 154)

In other words, the diffractive methodology is not just an alternative to critique as a practice in education. It's also a *childlike* method that de(con)structs and de/colonises education. In an interview with Hélène Cixous, Jacques Derrida (2019, p. 153) puts forward the idea that:

> Deconstruction is not critique, not only critique, because it doubts, it puts in question even problematisation, critique, doubt, skepticism, nihilism, etc. It is more childlike than every philosopher who claimed to start over *ab ovo*, from the beginning, no? All philosophers begin at the beginning. Descartes' radical doubt, Platonic wonder, and so forth, these are appeals to childhood.

A "childlike Derridaen deconstruction" of concepts has little to do with age. However, chronological children who are in the process of acquiring language can teach adults a great deal about how to philosophise (Murris, 2000). By disrupting the temporality of progress and disrupting humanist binaries such as Adult/Child, Culture/Nature, the diffractive methodology embraces *a childlike Baradian de(con)struction* by coming to concepts as if we are thinking them for the very first time, including the concept "infant".

Thinking the concept "infant" diffractively "outside of time", in the "now" (Chap. 2.5), disrupts developmental notions of progress both of individuals and of species ("savages"). This process of "racial differentiation" underlies our modern understanding of child (Nandy, 1987) and is used to justify treating adult Indigenous peoples and children as "intellectual and emotional primitives" (Murris & Reynolds, 2018). The child, the native, the continent of Africa is to be treated as a child, which articulates the idea that childhood is the logic of colonialism (Rollo, 2018). The "normal" developmental lines are diffractively de/constructed in the following image by cartoonist, Brandan Reynolds[18] (Fig. 4.1).

The undoing of "deep dualism" (Murris, 2016) by the childlike diffractive methodology is central to agential realism, and to its notion of de/colonising education. Chapter 3 describes how education's ontological organising principle is the Culture/Nature binary (Table 3.1)—a binary taught to children through representational bodies of knowledge. De/colonising education requires unlearning these

---

[18] From *The Posthuman Child Manifesto*, co-created by Murris and Reynolds (2018).

Fig. 4.1 Screenshot from *The Posthuman Child Manifesto*. Video and text available from: https://www.youtube.com/watch?v=ikN-LGhBawQ

concepts that are riddled with ontological binaries and engaging with nature/culture performative practices. An example from higher education gives a flavour of such teaching (Sect. 4.4).

4.3   On Questioning

De/colonising education involves disrupting the binary logic of western education *adults have learned* when they were younger. The practice of "cascading questions" is critical to diffraction methodology as introduced and diffracted through by Barad (especially their 2014 and 2018 articles) and other agential realists (e.g., Astrid Schrader, 2012). Cascading questions is what young people do until they start school and learn that you ask questions only when you do not know something. A know-it-all relationship towards truth tends to come with age, resulting from an educational system that values asking questions that educators and curriculum materials already know the answers to (Lipman et al., 1977). Asking questions tends to be seen in education as a sign of ignorance, of not knowing.

Walter Kohan (2015) proposes a childlike education that involves a particularly intense, nonnumerical relationship to time, as well as to truth. He suggests that asking questions slows down time, severing it from chronological time. He uses the term "childing" to describe the playful experimentation with questions, which young children's practices inspire. Yet, childing is not age-bound, but something all of us can do, also in higher education (Sect. 4.4).

Agential realism involves a re-turning to a childlike diffractive engagement with the world through questioning the meaning of concepts we tend to take for granted and investigating the work these concepts do, also politically. Agential realism helps build different (childlike) relationships "between" questions and answers. When tracing phenomena as part of the material analysis of objects, questions are met by further questions that cascade and generate further questioning. Questions such as whose knowledges count, the material conditions, and which concepts are assumed, help us examine what is already given before research gets underway, for example, what a brittlestar, a heron, or a stingray can teach (Sect. 4.1).

As educators, we learn about the important role assigned to questioning in agential realism by Barad's writing, and also by how Barad meets the questions asked by their audiences (halfway). YouTube videos of their talks and especially the Questions and Answers (Q & A) sessions afterwards are particularly insightful. Barad often praises the questioner and listens intently—making connections. When studying Barad's engagement in Q & A sessions, what is noticeable is how they (Barad) pay attention, not superficially or politely, but by listening carefully, doing justice to where the question might take the unfolding enquiry. Barad does not lecture or tell but teaches by doing diffractive material-discursive analyses themselves. Not for others to copy, but as a way of learning agential realism and changing the way the world worlds itself in its iterative becoming. This is how worlds change; asking questions about justice is part of producing data/empirical material (Juelskjær et al., 2021, p. 146). The key for Barad is 'to open up a space for asking the prior question, and then the prior question, and then again, the prior question', to provide an "onto-logical opening" (Barad & Gandorfer, 2021, p. 18). Asking questions is a matter of justice and response-ability. It provides openings for the human to respond, and also the other-than-human, including LEGO bricks,[19] animals, the dead, and whole fields of enquiry. As Donna Haraway (2016, p. 69) puts it: 'The task of the Speaker for the Dead is to bring the dead into the present, so as to make more response-able living and dying possible in times yet to come'.

Response-able pedagogies include allowing *fields of enquiry* to respond, not just humans. The risk otherwise is that questions invite responses that frustrate and are anti-educational because they don't do justice to the complexity of the investigations. They put the human (subject) in the position of the expert, thereby contradicting how agential realism reconfigures teaching and learning as a worlding practice (Chapter one). In conversation,[20] Barad commented that they were trained as a physicist and that they still have so much to learn, for example, by studying and working hard to read poststructuralist texts, including those by Derrida. Not referring to Deleuze is not out of lack of interest, but a lack of time. There are still so many projects Barad needs to do before they 'become compost'.

---

[19] See Chap. 3.

[20] See Footnote 17 in Chap. 1.

Taking agential realism seriously requires educators—including organisers of educational events—to build into their practices opportunities for enquiries to be provoked, nurtured, and taken diffractively into new directions. One way of doing this, is by making room for asking open, philosophical questions about core concepts that are either explicitly used by speakers or already assumed in their claims to knowledge and truth.

Agential realism can draw inspiration from childlike questioning and playful engagement with the world without essentialising, generalising, or romanticising chronological children. How can such prolific questioning in childhood be liberated from its spacetime container belonging to a particular chronological phase in a human's life? How can childlike questioning become a methodological feature of academic research in higher education (and not just for teacher education)? The questions provoked in turn by these questions generate exciting possibilities for the de/colonisation of education that includes the young human as a figuration, as a verb, as a performative practice in higher education.

4.4   On Teaching in Higher Education

You can walk around in concepts… I walk around in a sentence, I walk around in a word. A word, or even a letter, entails stories, different stories. (Barad in Barad & Gandorfer, 2021, p. 31)

Troubling Time/s and Ecologies of Nothingness (2018) is probably Barad's most relevant paper on memory. This diffractive paper on reworking the nature of time does not progress linearly. Barad diffracts through segments from a novella called *From Trinity to Trinity* (2010) by Japanese author Kyoko Hayashi, who, at the age of fourteen, witnessed the bombing of Nagasaki during which her classmates were killed. In a letter to Rui, a friend of thirty years and also a bomb survivor, Hayashi asks[21]:

The space in this world that the 52 people in my grade had occupied, the 52 spaces I cannot touch even if I extend my arms in a full embrace, what can I fill them with?

At the age of 14 Hayashi has lived, Barad says[22]:

29:23
through **an event that refuses to end**
29:25
that decays with time but will forever
29:28
continue to happen…

---

[21] From: https://apjjf.org/-Hayashi-Kyoko/2758/article.html; no page numbers.

[22] From the video transcript https://www.youtube.com/watch?v=bMVkg5UiRog&t=1736s.

Barad's diffractive storying (of Hayashi's story) doesn't only make us wonder what constitutes an event, but also what memory is. These two concepts are critical in my work with university students. In one course, we start by inviting the students to remember a moment in time in their professional practice when they weren't sure what to do. An event that 'refuses to end'. So, we need to walk around in the concepts involved, slow things down, enquire, avoid giving definitions, connect concepts with others, keep returning to them, compost them and tell stories. We let the questions cascade and turn teaching "upside down". As educators, we aren't there to provide the answers but to make room (even in Zoom) to ask questions collaboratively in *communities of enquiry*—the pedagogy of Philosophy with Children (Rollins Gregory et al., 2017). By not pinning down meaning with a priori definitions, such opportunities build communities (of enquiry) and simultaneously already assume that thinking is a collaborative practice. It also involves normalising disagreement and a different doing of difference as always "within" and not "without" (Chap. 1.2).

The programme that serves as an example in this chapter is a master's course on the ethics and politics of education at a university in Northern Finland. There were around sixty students from Education Science and Early Childhood Education in 2021. They are primarily Finnish home language speakers and not fluent in English, although this compulsory course is taught in English. All teaching took place via Zoom because of the pandemic. Few students have their cameras open as it is not a university requirement to do so. It is the first time we co-teach this course, and students have given their permission to have their assignments used anonymously for research purposes. Inspired by Karen Barad's explicit reference to their own teaching of higher education students in Santa Cruz (a Science & Justice Graduate Training Program), we provided the following hand-out, which we had adapted to our purposes. It is an edited and summarised version of pages 135–140 of an interview with Barad in Juelskjær et al.'s excellent book *Dialogues on Agential Realism* (2021).

Course Ethics and Politics in Education 2021
Diffractive journal:

You will be working on Google in groups of three throughout this course. This journaling process will support the below assessment process. You will be assigned a group at the start, randomly assigned.

The task
Analysis of a case-study of your own professional dilemma

1. Write a short narrative of the dilemma.
2. Select an object and trace it: It can be any object—found or made or even human.

    a. You need to get to know everything you can about the object, paying particular attention to who is saying what about it—that is, making sure they attend to the fact that different experts (those who get to claim expertise according to particular standards of what constitutes knowledge) will have different things to say about a given object; this is importantly true of other stakeholders as well (including workers who produce particular objects, those affected by, say, the mining of particular minerals that make up component parts, etc.). It's a matter of getting to know the object, and you need to get to know it in the most technical ways and also to understand the various and sometimes competing stakes that people have in it, both as producers and users. Focus on getting to know the object, scientifically, technically, socially, politically, affectively and so on.

   b.   create a dynamic map, performance, sketch, video, dance, sculpture of clay….

        Still or moving images constructed during the seminars will be the core of this assignment as a material means of sensing/making sense, getting a feel for, the various entanglements your specific object in (2) is entangled with and try to visually trace these. Also make clear the weight of the different entanglements. What is less or more important and why is this?

3.   Begin an analysis of the phenomenon (the object is part of) by focusing in on two or three of the many and diverse apparatuses of bodily production that help constitute the phenomenon. Please note: the very constitution of matter is itself political; matter is precisely not thingness and phenomena are not objects, but are always shot through with gender, race, labour, money, etc. In fact, at the end of the analysis the object can be crossed out.

A short, written essay (max 1000 words) needs to engage with the political and ethical dimensions of 1–3, thereby giving insight in how differences are made and unmade. The main criteria for assessment are originality and deep engagement with the (guest)lectures and theories that show the difference the course has made for your ideas about the ethics and politics of education and educational practices.

    This assignment can be submitted as an mp3 or 4 as well.

At the heart of the exercise is the tracing of an object as phenomenon. In 2021, we used the analysis of Zuko playing with Lego bricks (see Chap. 3) as an illustration. Each student chose their own object that was somehow entangled with the narrative of their professional dilemma. Their objects were incredibly varied: e.g., a pencil, a comforter, a door, a shoe, an iPhone, an aeroplane, a doll. Guest lecturers from Finland, Brazil, England, and Australia presented various topics (e.g., care, gender, environmental education, black childhood, philosophical questioning) that helped the students tell their stories—moving from object to phenomenon—using different "lenses". One student shares the following memory of a dilemma with the stick as the "main stakeholder":

Back in 2018 I was working as an intern in a pre-school group of thirteen children. It was late autumn, just a few weeks before the first snow falls. You could feel the frost in the air. All the leaves had fallen from the trees. It was a cold, bright day when our group went for a walking trip into a forest. We walked in a long line, the teacher in the front, me in the middle and the group assistant as the last, with children between us. On our way back, one of the children picked up a stick and carried it in an upward position. Like a spear, or a flag. I was walking behind that child, keeping an eye on the group. Suddenly another child yelled a bit; they got a scratch on their cheek from the stick that the other child was carrying. I told them both to stop and looked at the child's scratch. It was nothing to worry about, just a very light reddish mark. I bet it did hurt, though. When your cheeks are cold, any scratch will hurt. The child carrying a stick didn't seem to care much about the accident. I had told the child to be very careful with the stick, and they had been, but the child had walked pass the other child and the stick got too close and made a scratch. I didn't think it was wrong to carry that stick in the manner that child did, but there's this little possibility that accidents like this could happen. So, the stick had to be left behind and apologies were said. We kept on walking back to the daycare centre.

In the yard, I told the teacher what had happened. The teacher thought that it'd be better not to tell the parent that their child got a scratch. I asked why, because I didn't see any reason for not telling. I had been taught that if children got any marks on their skin (bruises, scratches, etc.) you should tell their parents where that came from. The teacher explained that the reason was to avoid the parent's possible reaction, saying it was usual for that parent to "overreact over little things". I still told the parent though, when they came to pick up their child. I felt like it was the right thing to do. The parent did get a little furious and suspicious about what had happened and thought immediately that their child had been in a fight with the other child and that's why they ended up getting a scratch. I made sure that the parent understood that the scratch was an accident, and the children did not get into a fight or anything. The other child had simply walked a bit too close to their child while proudly carrying a stick. The parent understood and calmed down. I felt like the parent had expected that it was their child's fault.

Maybe they had heard a similar story many times and assumed this could be just a new one to be added to the list: that their child had been in a fight with another child. But should a teacher lie to avoid a parent's negative reaction?

The student who submitted this assignment continues by asking several questions raised by her dilemma. The stick is a familiar and often treasured object for many children. Banning it from the daycare centre just in case a child might get scratched raised ethical and political questions for the student. Interestingly, she didn't choose the stick as her object to trace, but a door. What it is made off, its aesthetics, how it creates insides and outsides (who/what is kept in and out?), how it can be locked with a key, how it was manufactured, its history, the metaphorical use of doors, also in films and literature. How a door can keep you away from what you 'desperately want to reach: freedom, an answer, or an opportunity'.

As lecturers we don't know beforehand what the exact content of this course is going to be. We have some ideas for provocations, but we make room for the students' stories and try to respond to them by asking questions. As "clairvoyant stingrays" we try to "anticipate messages" when they haven't arrived yet (see Sect. 4.1). Here is a brief "snippet" of our teaching after a guest lecture by Karen Malone from Swinburne

Fig. 4.2 Video clip from
Karen Malone's article
*Worlding with Kin
Diffracting Childfish
Sensorial Ecological
Encounters through Moving
Image* (2019). Open access

University of Technology as part of the course. The students had read Malone's open-source article called *Worlding with Kin* (2019) in a Special Issue on *Videography and Decolonizing Childhood*. During the lecture, we watch the clip together (Fig. 4.2).[23] It is a short encounter between a young human and a fish in an aquarium. Karen Malone spoke about how she was 'sensing ecologically' as a tool in her research and how examples such as the one in the video help her 'imagine how very young children encounter nonhuman relations prior to language acquisition. That is, how bodies find ways to be with animals, plants, water, and materials' (Fig. 4.2).

The intra-active diffractive journal we keep as lecturers is a way of communicating between the sessions with the students. It reads:

> On Friday, it worked out better to follow on from Karen's lecture by letting them ask questions after working first in break out rooms…I haven't seen any work on the diffractive journals yesterday so why not ask them to write a short dialogue (Finnish or English) between the girl, the fish and the glass that separates them using some of their questions below? I will look for some quotes from Vinciane Despret (*On Asking the Right Questions*).

However, the idea of writing the dialogue from different perspectives (fish, girl, or the glass) is not taken up by the students. And we sense that maybe another idea might work. We use the *Worlding with Kin* clip as a provocation for cascading questions on a shared file on the university site. Here are some of their questions, deliberately left "untouched" (by us educators) as they show the different ways of going about the invitation.

Fish:
Miltä lapsi näyttää kalan silmissä lasin takana? (What does the child look like to the fish?)
Mikä tuo olento on? (What is that creature?)
Mitä tuijotat? (What are you looking at?)

---

[23] You can also download it here: https://brill.com/view/journals/vjep/4/1/article-p69_69.xml

Miten pääsen lasin toiselle puolelle? (How can I get to the other side of the glass?)
Mitä toisella puolella on? (What is there on the other side?
Miksi olen täällä? (Why am I here?)
Olisiko sinulla ruokaa? (Do you have food?)

Child:
Leikkiikö tuo kala minun kanssani? (Is this fish playing with me?)
Pääseekö kala pois akvaariosta? (Can the fish leave the aquarium?)
Miksi kala on akvaariossa? (Why is the fish in the aquarium?)
Onko kalalla perhettä? (Does the fish have a family?)
Entä lapsia? (How about children?)
Miksi kala on yksin? (Why is the fish alone?)
Onko kala yksinäinen? (Is the fish lonely?)
Voiko kala olla minun kaverini? (Can the fish be my friend?)
Mitä kalan kanssa voisi tehdä? (What can I do with the fish?)

Fish: How it feels to live in freedom? Fish: What is that and why is it disturbing me? Child: How did you get there? Child: Why is the fish in aquarium and not in the sea? Child: What kind of fish is that? Child: Is the fish ok and feeling good in the aquarium? Fish: How can you live outside of water? Fish: Why is the child in aquarium? Fish from us: Why do you capture me? Fish from us: How does it feel to be free? Fish from us: Are you captured too?

- Is the fish used as an entertainment /education tool for people in this case? Do we as human have the right to use animal that way? Do we feel comfortable when we being used as examples for other people by being locked in a limited space?
- Are aquariums ethical?
- Does the appearance of people affect animals' normal life? Is this a normal environment for animals to live in (light, noise, interruption of human)?
- Does the fish want to communicate with child?
- Does the child realize that the fish is held in captivity?
- How can they communicate?
- Is the fish happy?
- What does the fish think?

> Who are you?
> What do you think about?
> Are you happy?
> Can you get me out of here?

Child's questions:

- Does the fish see us in the same way that we see it?
- How can the fish breathe under water?
- Do you (fish) have a family?
- Are you alone?
- What do you do there (during summer/holiday/night etc.)?

- Are you afraid of me?

Fish's questions:

- How can you live without water?
- How do you move like that?
- Do you have to be afraid of those who are bigger than you?
- Are you going to eat me?

After reading their many questions and being moved by their engagement, we sensed it might work to diffract through another "language" (Sect. 4.1), and that it would be powerful to re-turn to the aquarium. This time not in small groups, but plenary. Making the most of meeting in Zoom, we introduced the following provocation, inspired by the 24 h Choir by Julian Day, an interdisciplinary composer and writer. (https://www.youtube.com/watch?v=OMyE5ix58SM&list= PLV_R_Am5XBnmg9CPL8iGqBqn02mEFaAhO).

After watching the first minutes to get the idea, we asked the students to turn their camera off and while watching Fig. 4.2 improvise a communal choir inspired by the child-fish encounter. One person starts to make a sound, and then people take turns, listening carefully to one another. We sing, hum, whistle, heavily breathe, moan, laugh at the meeting between fish, girl, adult, water, glass, camera, student, Zoom, etc. At first it didn't work to keep the sound going, but with the second communal effort we manage to create a very haunting sound with voices from the deep as we move our bodyminds back into the aquarium. The effect was co-created by Tuure Tammi, the co-lecturer of the course, who changed the speed of the original recording and then with the use of echo and equaliser recorded the process onto a magnetic tape—turning the recording of the students' "choir" into a soundscape (Fig. 4.3). He had prepared it for the next (last) lecture of the course. We listened to the recording together, without speaking and then one-by-one left the Zoom room. This event is to be dis/continued.

4.5   On Assessment

Teaching a course in higher education gives a flavour of agential realism in action and the difference it makes (Sect. 4.4). But how can we assess such a course, also diffractively? Criticality is, of course, very much part of the academic life and is a practice that educators in the academy should familiarise their students

Fig. 4.3 Haunted *Worlding with Kin* soundscape. Co-created by Tuure Tammi. Published with his permission

with. Criticality also underpins teaching and assessment in all phases of education. Following on from the difference between critique and diffraction (Sect. 4.1), the kind of critique Barad (2014, p. 187, ftn 63) embraces are those put forward by Marx, Nietzsche, and Foucault. How diffractive analysis and critique differ in their ontology and temporality is important for assessment: the latter (critique) is 'operating in a mode of disclosure, exposure and demystification' (destruction), while diffraction is 'a form of affirmative engagement' creating new 'patterns of understanding-becoming' (construction and deconstruction) (Barad, 2014, p. 187, ftn 63). Barad's scholarship has inspired me to put together the following table with de(con)structive performative practices for assessing texts (Table 4.1). However, the line in between doesn't set up a binary opposition between diffraction and reflection, because as Barad (2007, p. 466) points out: 'even a [Cartesian] cut that breaks things apart does not cause a separation but furthers the entanglement!'.

Table 4.1 Agential realism and the differences "between" diffractive and reflective assessment of texts

Agential realism	
Reflective assessment	Diffractive assessment
Educator is the expert, has an overview of the fields in question and uses his/her/their superior knowledge to make comments and help 'fix' or 'strengthen' the text that tends to be in words (and English often privileged)	Educator and student are in conversation producing new insights (also for the educator). This conversation can be through a multiplicity of languages: words, dance, paint, music, video, etc., diffracting through one another
Cartesian cut Breaks apart in different directions. The comments don't add connections but use difference to be critical (through identity as foundational) to replace, rather than affirm and add, in order to produce a new insight (i.e., new for both: educator and student)	*Agential cut* Cutting-together apart; there is no outside or view from nowhere Assessment is a re-turning, not something that happened in the past as closed. Comments add because ideas and texts are porous without boundaries. Moving away from identity and who said what and when, because ideas are always already entangled with past, present, and future ideas (and mothers, children, pet animals, sea, wind, etc., that made those ideas possible)
Assumes binaries Words, things, and people are separate ontological entities. Reflection is an inner mental activity where an educator supposedly takes a step back, distancing him/herself from the topic at hand This makes power-producing binaries possible, such as: expert/novice, insider/outsider, academic/practitioner, theory/practice	*De(con)structs binaries* Disrupts power-producing binaries that thrive on identity. Regards the human not as an ontological, but as a political category Importantly, it disrupts the theory/practice binary (conceptual/empirical), so the theoretical and practical are read through one another. Practice is not an application of theory as so often assumed in assessment
Representational Words mirror nature, reality, etc. (culture/nature binary presupposed) Assumes educators can have an overview of the field, can identify gaps and what is lacking in students Even in reflexive research, the idea is to interrogate and identify how one's own self is implicated in an assessment exercise	*Non/representational* Words and things, nature and culture are all entangled and can't be re-presented. No big picture, or map, or overview is possible as part of an assignment Assessment is not a regurgitation (a repeat) of the "content" the educator has indicated as important to learn. The focus is on the new produced intra-actively, also through the material (e.g., technology)

(continued)

Table 4.1 (continued)

Agential realism	
Reflective assessment	Diffractive assessment
Outsider perspective	*'Insider' perspective*
A perspective from a distance, as if the educator is ontologically separate from the text she is reading using criteria that are external to the work itself and imposed from the outside. It is assumed that judgement about texts can be objective. The kind of objectivity that assumes the objective/subjective binary (with intersubjectivity as alternative)	The educator is ontologically part of the world and the text. She thinks *with* the text as if she is entangled with it and many factors influence her reading—many unbeknown to her (e.g., the atmosphere)
In teacher education, we tend to use psychological, political, historical, and socio-cultural theories for reflective assessments	Redefinition of objectivity. Doing justice to the complexity of the world that should be understood transdisciplinary. When diffracting, the perspectives of other disciplines (geography, biology, etc.) are woven through the topic at hand. The entities that have been erased and ignored from social sciences are made visible (also at quantum level)
Being an outsider is meant here ontologically not epistemologically	Being an insider is meant here ontologically, not epistemologically. There is no outside ontologically
Knowing is mental	*Knowing is performative*
A cognitive process that takes place inside the human; separated from the body (emotion/affect)	An iterative practice that leaves marks on bodies and sediments the world
	No cognition/affect binary is assumed
Text is object	*Text is porous*
Reading an assignment is a reflective process that involves going back to the text as if it is a thing in the past that is finished and static (unilinear time assumed) and an independently existing object for the educator	Reading an assignment (or assessing a transmodal text, e.g., a dance) is a dynamic process of *thinking together with and through the text* as an emergent, open, in/determinate process
	Paying attention to the differences and the fine-grained details that matter
Responsibility (individual ability)	*Response-ability*
Educators are individuals with rights and responsibilities for their assessments. They can be anonymous (sometimes even heralded as better, less biased), Paying attention to individual creativity, originality, and autonomy. Copying and plagiarism is punished	The educator makes it possible for the 'other' to respond (including the other-than-human). A transindividual commitment to *undo* the injustices committed to those who are (also) no longer there (as well as our 'own' childhood 'selves'). Paying attention to existences excluded. Always political

4.6 On

4.6.1 On K/Not

Nothingness. The void. An absence of matter. The blank page. Utter silence. No thing, no thought, no awareness. Complete ontological insensibility. Shall we utter some words about nothingness? What is there to say? How to begin? How can anything be said about nothing without violating its very nature, perhaps even its conditions of possibility? Isn't any utterance about nothingness always already a performative breach of that which one means to address? Have we not already said too much simply in pronouncing its name? Perhaps we should let the emptiness speak for itself. (Barad, 2012, p. 4)

References

Barad, K. (2007). *Meeting the universe halfway: Quantum physics and the entanglement of matter and meaning*. Duke University Press.
Barad, K. (2010). Quantum entanglements and hauntological relations of inheritance: Dis/continuities, spacetime enfoldings, and justice-to-come. *Derrida Today, 3*(2), 240–68. https://doi.org/10.3366/drt.2010.0206
Barad, K. (2011). Nature's Queer Performativity. *Qui Parle, 19*(2), 121–158.
Barad, K. (2012). What is the measure of nothingness? Infinity, virtuality, justice/Was ist das Maß des Nichts? Unendlichkeit, Virtualität, Gerechtigkeit, DOCUMENTA (13): 100 Notes—100 Thoughts / 100 Notizen—100 Gedanken I Book N°099 (English & German edition, 2012).
Barad, K. (2014). Diffracting diffractions: Cutting together-apart. *Parallax, 20*(3), 168–187.
Barad, K. (2017). What flashes up: Theological-political-scientific fragments. In C. Keller & M.-J. Rubenstein (Eds.), *Entangled worlds: Religion, science, and new materialisms* (pp. 21–88). Fordham University Press.
Barad, K., & Gandorfer, D. (2021). Political desirings: Yearnings for mattering (,) differently. *Theory & Event, 24*(1), 14–66.
Battersby, C. (1998). *The phenomenal woman: Feminist metaphysics and the patterns of identity*. New York: Routledge.
Bhattacharya, K. (2009). Othering research, researching the other: De/colonizing approaches to qualitative inquiry. In J. Smart (Ed.), *Higher education: Handbook of theory and research* (Vol. 24, pp. 105–150). Springer.
Cixous, H., & Derrida, J. (2019). On deconstruction and childhood (P. Kamuf, Trans.). *The Oxford Literary Review, 41*(2), 149–159.
Haraway, D. (1988). Situated Knowledges: The science question in feminism and the privilege of partial perspective. *Feminist Studies, 14*, 575–599.
Haraway, D. (2016). *Staying with the trouble: Making kin in the Chthulucene*. Duke University Press.
Hayashi, K. (2010). *From trinity to trinity*. Station Hill.
Heidegger, M. (1979). *Sein und Zeit*. Max Niemeyer.
Juelskjær, M., Plauborg, H., & Adrian, S. (2021). *Dialogues on agential realism: Engaging in worldings through research practice*. Routledge.
Kohan, W. (2015). *The inventive schoolmaster*. Sense.
Lipman, M., Sharp, A. M., & Oscanyan, F. S. (1977). *Philosophy in the classroom*. Philadelphia: Temple University Press.
McGregor, K. (2020). Material flows: Patriarchal structures and the menstruating teacher. *Gender and Education, 32*(3), 382–394.
Murris, K. (2000). Can children do philosophy? *Journal of Philosophy of Education, 34*(2), 261–279.

Murris, K. (2016). *The posthuman child: Educational transformation through philosophy with picturebooks*. Contesting Early Childhood Series (G. Dahlberg & P. Moss, Eds.). Routledge.

Murris, K. (2017). Reconfiguring educational relationality in education: The educator as pregnant stingray. *Journal of Education, 69*, 117–138.

Murris, K. (2018). Posthuman child and the diffractive teacher: Decolonizing the nature/culture binary. In A. Cutter-Mackenzie, K. Malone, E. Barratt Hacking (Eds.), *Research handbook on childhoodnature: Assemblages of childhood and nature research* (pp. 1–25). Springer International Handbooks of Education.

Murris, K. (2021). The 'missing peoples' of critical posthumanism and new materialism. In K. Murris (Ed.), *Navigating the postqualitative, new materialist and critical posthumanist terrain across disciplines: An introductory guide* (pp. 62–85). Routledge.

Murris, K., & Bozalek, V. (2019a). Diffraction and response-able reading of texts: The relational ontologies of Barad and Deleuze. *International Journal for Qualitative Studies in Education, 32*(7), 872–886. https://doi.org/10.1080/09518398.2019.1609122

Murris, K., & Bozalek, V. (2019b). Diffracting diffractive readings of texts as methodology: Some propositions. *Educational Philosophy and Theory, 51*(14), 1504–1517. https://doi.org/10.1080/00131857.2019.1570843

Murris, K., & Kohan, W. (2020). Troubling troubled school times: Posthuman multiple temporalities. *International Journal of Qualitative Studies in Education.* https://doi.org/10.1080/09518398.2020

Murris, K. [Project: Decolonizing Early Childhood Discourses], & Reynolds, B. (Producer). (2018, September 5). *A manifesto posthuman child: De/colonising childhood through reconfiguring the human* [Video]. Youtube. https://www.youtube.com/watch?v=ikN-LGhBawQ

Nandy, A. (1987). Reconstructing childhood: A critique of the ideology of adulthood. In A. Nandy (Ed.), *Traditions, tyranny and utopias: Essays in the politics of awareness* (pp. 56–77). Oxford University Press.

Nxumalo, F. (2020). Situating Indigenous and Black childhoods in the Anthropocene. In A. Cutter-Mackenzie, K. Malone, & E. Barratt Hacking (Eds.), *International research handbook on childhoodnature: Assemblages of childhood and nature research* (pp. 535–557). Springer International Handbooks of Education.

Patel, L. (2016). *Decolonising educational research: From ownership to answerability*. Routledge.

Rivers, P. (2017). Decolonizing the toilet. *Briarpatch Magazine.* See: https://briarpatchmagazine.com/articles/view/decolonizing-the-toilet

Rollins Gregory, M., Haynes, J., & Murris, K. (Eds.). (2017). *The Routledge international handbook of philosophy for children* (pp. 43–53). Routledge.

Rollo, T. (2018). Feral children: Settler colonialism, progress, and the figure of the child. *Settler Colonial Studies, 8*(1), 60–71. https://doi.org/10.1080/2201473X.2016.1199826

Schrader, A. (2012). Haunted measurements: Demonic work and time in experimentation. *Differences: A Journal of Feminist Cultural Studies, 23*(3), 119–160.

Semetsky, I. R. (2015). *Edusemiotics: Semiotic philosophy as educational foundation*. Routledge.

Smith, L. T. (1999). *Decolonizing methodologies: Research and indigenous peoples*. Zed Books.

Snaza, N. (2015). Toward a genealogy of educational humanism. In N. Snaza & J. A. Weaver (Eds.), *Posthumanism and educational research* (pp. 17–30). Routledge.

Sundberg, J. (2014). Decolonizing posthumanist geographies. *Cultural Geographies, 21*(1), 33–47.

Tuck, E., Mckenzie, M., & McCoy, K. (2014) Land education: Indigenous, post-colonial, and decolonizing perspective on place and environmental education research. *Environmental Education Research, 20*(1). https://doi.org/10.1080/13504622.2013.877708

UNICEF & World Health Organization. (2018). *Drinking water, sanitation, and hygiene at school: Global baselines report*. Online: https://news.un.org/en/story/2018/08/1017812

WaterAid. (2018). *The crisis in the classroom: The state of the world's toilets 2018* [report]. Online: https://www.wateraid.org/us/sites/g/files/jkxoof291/files/World%20Toilet%20Day%20Report%202018.pdf

Watts, V. (2013). Indigenous place-thought and agency amongst humans and non humans (First Woman and Sky Woman go on a European world tour!). *Decolonization: Indigeneity, Education & Society, 2*(1), 20–34.

Zhao, W. (2019). Daoist onto-un-learning as a radical form of study: Re-imagining learning and study from an Eastern perspective. *Studies in Philosophy and Education, 38*(3), 261–273.

Printed by Printforce, United Kingdom